INFLATION
A
WORLD-WIDE
DISASTER

INFLATION
A
WORLD-WIDE
DISASTER

Irving S. Friedman

HOUGHTON MIFFLIN COMPANY · BOSTON

To

YALE UNIVERSITY
and
ALL SOULS COLLEGE, OXFORD
for providing
the inspiring environment
in which this book
was written

Preface

Inflation was still regarded in the United States as a minor problem in mid-1970. My own conviction was that the United States would soon be immersed in a major inflationary problem and that the public in the United States, as elsewhere, was ill-prepared to understand what was at stake and ill-prepared for the inevitable debate on governmental policies to meet the situation. For years I had wanted to write a book on the subject that would assist the general public and their leaders in the United States and elsewhere in evaluating inflation and in considering alternative policies that would be advocated by politicians, economists, and others. I had no desire to write a technical book for monetary experts, or a "popular" book in economics; but rather to approach the problem from a broad social and political, as well as economic, viewpoint. Only in this way could modern inflation be understood. I hoped that students of social science would find the book revealing and that it would challenge them to apply their research and theoretical skills to this very real challenge.

Fortunately, the opportunity to have a sabbatical year, in 1970 and 1971, away from the World Bank as a Visiting

Fellow at All Souls, Oxford, and Yale University made this writing possible.

In the meantime, inflationary pressures mounted to a point at which they could no longer be ignored. The most dramatic change and most publicized was in the United States — most dramatic because it led to a complete reversal in national economic management in 1971 and most publicized because it was the United States. Inflation, however, is at least as serious a problem in nearly all countries outside of the United States and more serious in many. Everywhere, the corrosive effects of inflation frustrate governments' attempts to reach modern social and economic objectives and eat away the fabric which we call society and civilization.

This is not a "doomsday" book. I do not regard inflation as inevitable. I do regard it as evidence of universal economic mismanagement, as governments have not yet learned how to govern modern societies. I do believe that in an environment of continuing inflation modern societies will fail.

This book has no bibliography, no footnotes, no statistical tables, and no charts. I have tried very hard to avoid technical language familiar to the expert but puzzling to most. The book represents my attempt to generalize from actual experiences, which have included dealing with economic problems of countries for thirty years. During these years important contributions have been made by scholars to our understanding of economic and social behavior. I hope that this book will encourage its readers to delve more deeply and scholars to research more deeply into the facts and to re-examine their hypotheses and approaches to inflation.

The book could not have been written without the benefit

of the countless people over the years with whom I have had the chance to examine and exchange views on the economic and social problems of their countries, as together we sought viable solutions. I am deeply indebted to these friends. Many of them are on the staff of the World Bank, the International Monetary Fund, and other national and international agencies. None of them can, however, be held responsible in any way for my views.

I also wish to express my gratitude to the many scholars at Yale and All Souls with whom I had the opportunity to discuss various aspects of inflation during my stays there. They included particularly Professors Orcutt, Triffin, Wallich, and Ranis at Yale, and Professors Mathias, Sir John Hicks, Lord Balogh, Streeten, and Stuvel at Oxford.

I would also like to express my gratitude to various persons who, at one stage or another, read the manuscript. They include Alice Orcutt Nakamura, Lawrence Coore, V. V. Bhatt, Thomas D. Finney, Marvin Bordelon, William Ryan, Kenneth Friedman, Kanella Vasiliades, and Andrew M. Overby. Arthur E. Tiemann and his staff at the World Bank were most helpful in providing background statistical information. Elinor Yudin was particularly helpful in commenting on and editing the manuscript. Since the book was a family venture, I would like finally to thank my children and, especially, my wife Edna.

Contents

Postscript as Prologue

AS THIS BOOK was being prepared for press in mid-February 1973, the latest international monetary crisis was taking place. In early February, Italy and Switzerland had to go on to a floating-rate system. By mid-February, the situation had reached crisis proportions: the U.S. dollar was again devalued — this time by 10 percent, raising the price of gold to $42.22 per ounce. Japan floated its currency, the yen.

How enduring this will prove remains unknown. Again the international monetary system has proven vulnerable. It will continue to do so as long as expectations of simultaneous persistent inflation in the developed countries raise serious doubts about the viability of any existing pattern of exchange rates. Temporary welcome improvements may materialize from the changes made in crisis, but they cannot be expected to endure. Only when countries stop regarding inflation as "under control" because its rate is reduced from the higher level of an immediately preceding period can lasting improvement result. The crucial factor continues to be the end of inflationary expectations, not the magnitude of the new rates of inflation.

When we face up to the deep roots of inflationary expectations which result from persistent inflation, we will
find solutions. Then both a viable international monetary
system and viable societies will be possible.

I

Introduction

1

Perspective
on Persistent Inflation

During the last three decades, country after country has tried to cope with the problem of continuously rising prices and wages. Temporary successes have been achieved in some countries but the general record is one of repeated failures. Governments have proved incapable of providing solutions that are politically and socially acceptable. Instead, they have pursued policies that have strengthened inflationary trends and have led to the nearly universal conviction that inflation is incvitable and that governments cannot, or should not, bring rising-price trends to an end. People everywhere seek, in their own ways, to protect themselves against the effects of these trends, and, if possible, to profit from their existence.

The failure of governments to deal with these problems is not due to a lack of interest or concern. It is at least partly due to the failure to understand the basic cause of inflation in modern societies and to an inadequate appreciation of its social, economic, and political effects — which I summarize as "societal" effects.

For many centuries, the phenomenon of rising prices, called inflation, was essentially temporary. It occurred in

many countries for special reasons, mainly major wars such
as the Napoleonic wars and the U.S. Civil War, and because
of occasional increases in the world supply of gold and silver,
the principal money of the world, after strikes were made
and mines opened in California, Alaska, South Africa, Australia, Canada, and elsewhere.

The old civilizations in the Western Hemisphere, "discovered" by the Europeans, proved to have extraordinarily
large supplies and a capacity for new output of precious
metals which greatly augmented existing European supplies
and output. In the sixteenth century European society was
rocked by these large increases in its money supplies. Prices
rose in one European country after another as these metals
found their way from Spain and elsewhere to other countries.
The problems of money and prices at this period of history
came to the forefront of attention of thinkers and political
leaders. Everything had to adjust to the new monetary conditions — including the Church's attitude toward what was a
"just" price and what were "usurious" interest rates. Some
nations, like England, and new social and economic classes
thrived under the changed conditions. Some traditional
groups and institutions, such as the Church, adapted well, but
others, such as the Spanish society and government, never did,
and declined in international stature and influence.

Since the sixteenth century, however, inflation has been
neither persistent nor all-pervasive, until the last three decades. In the intervening period, inflation continued to be
feared by those who favored economic and social stability;
many had inherited the sixteenth-century experience with
inflation and its disruptive effects in their folklore. Others

welcomed inflation. They were equally aware of its disruptive social effects, but favored drastic changes in their societies. For many, inflation became synonymous with periods of prosperity, welcomed as a stimulant to industry and commerce. Those who held wealth in forms which lost their purchasing power as prices rose — like loans to individuals or government bonds — were hostile to inflationary trends, even temporary ones. Those who were in debt and those who held wealth in other forms, like land, often were content when such trends appeared. But, with occasional exceptions, the fact that inflation in these centuries repeatedly proved temporary and limited in the number of countries simultaneously experiencing these trends deprived inflation of the great significance which it had had in the sixteenth century.

The most important legacies of these post-sixteenth centuries were certain ideas: that rising prices were associated with prosperity; that their causes were very largely to be found in increases in gold and silver, or the supply of money; that inflation, if and when it occurred, would prove to be temporary; that its effects would not be world-wide, nor were they likely to be important socially and politically, as well as economically. Other economic developments, like the Industrial Revolution, were clearly much more important. Inflation was neither difficult to handle nor, on balance, vitally harmful. Russia after the Revolution and Germany after World War I were seen by some as exceptions, raising fears that explosive inflation might be a major cause of revolutionary upheavals. Clearly, rampant inflation was a consequence of these revolutionary situations which in turn made the restoration of stable sociopolitical conditions much more difficult. These explosions, therefore, did not teach people to fear inflation as a major destroyer of societies since inflation was not primarily a cause of such disruptions but rather was an effect.

Thus the twentieth century was intellectually ill-prepared — and still is — to understand the modern phenomenon of persistent inflation, its world-wide scope and its societal causes and societal effects. It does not see persistent inflation as a potential destroyer of societies; it does not probe its causes to get much beyond an understanding of the relation between money and prices. Yet the persistent world-wide inflation that now exists is stronger and more pervasive than the sixteenth-century inflation. It is transmitted from country to country as depression was in the 1930s. If inflation were temporary, its causes and effects would be easily explained in terms of money and prices. Its control would be relatively simple. But the persistence of inflation makes it necessary to look deeper for causes and effects. Unless these are understood, we will not understand why persistent inflation is a destroyer of modern societies and we cannot know how to begin to deal with this problem effectively.

The investigation of the social and political as well as economic effects of persistent inflation entails our entering into unexplored territories. It is not simply to look more intensively at the traditional problem of temporary inflation. It is to probe a phenomenon which has many causes and effects common with temporary inflation. But persistent inflation is so different that there is a greater danger, as experience has repeatedly indicated: to tackle persistent inflation in the same way as temporary inflation is not only to invite failure, but to make the problem much worse and more difficult to solve.

Since this book deals with a world-wide phenomenon, it is based on experiences of countries all over the world during the last three decades. It makes no claim to having exhausted the analysis of causes and effects, nor to offering conclusive solutions for each country. It does try to direct attention to this major world condition, indicate how persistent inflation might be better understood and appreciated, and how it might more successfully be tackled.

The book's approach is societal, because the problem is societal, not in the narrow sense that all people are affected and involved; in this sense the discovery of a new medicine or the invention of a new camera is societal. The approach is societal because the causes of persistent inflation are just as much social and political as economic; so are its effects. Solutions, therefore, have to deal with these social causes and aim to eliminate the unwanted societal effects. It means that it is a subject not only for economists, or even only for all social scientists; it involves all who participate in the political process. This is inherent in the phenomenon of persistent inflation. Because of this, the book explores political and social as well as economic origins of existing persistent inflation and, similarly, tries to trace some of its political and social as well as economic effects.

What must be seen is that the effects of persistent inflation are devastating for all kinds of societies. None is immune. To accept the persistent rising trends as inevitable is to accept the inevitability of the devastating effects — devastating because they attack and erode the fundamentals on which any organized society rests, irrespective of political and social ideology and structures. Persistent inflation is a universal solvent of organized societies. The ills of such inflation fall most heavily on the poorest, but the great majority of people are increasingly harmed in many different ways. Among its victims are national objectives of satisfactory levels of growth, employment, and income distribution.

But the causes of persistent inflation are not irreversible. Their harmful effects can be eliminated and the achievement of other national objectives made more feasible. Their reversal does call for a drastic re-evaluation of our approaches to social and economic problems and new political institutions. Minor or even major alterations of existing practices may not do the job; persistent inflation is too deeply rooted and its effects veined throughout society because we have delayed so long in even recognizing the problem.

Therefore this book is a call to action based on an analysis of the causes and effects of persistent inflation as experienced by countries throughout the world and an examination of feasible corrective measures. If the problems continue to be underestimated either in the strength of their roots or the harm of their effects, or in the difficulties in achieving successful cures, we will have to live with the costly consequences. For we cannot expect effective political action — which will have to be different in each of the countries — to be taken unless the depth and scope of the problem are much more fully understood and the feasible political alternatives explored and debated, and critical choices made.

I hope that this book will help to make people aware of the problem in its fullness. If this happens, the world may be spared much additional damage and suffering. The environmental movement waited decades before remedial action began. It was not until man achieved the "miracle" of changing the color of the heavens and blotting out the sun that the warnings given decades ago were heeded. Effective action to solve the problem of persistent inflation may need to wait for intolerable hardships to great sections of people in all countries before political leadership can fulfill its role of guiding people through economic and social crises without destroying the fabric and continuity of civilization. Serious hardships are already being experienced by very many; the sooner the seriousness of the problem is appreciated, the fewer people will suffer. All of us everywhere are involved. We can only attempt to avoid that bitter experience be the only effective teacher.

II

The Roots of
Modern Inflation

2

The Century of Inflation

Continuously rising prices and wages — persistent inflation — is a world-wide phenomenon which has existed for more than a generation. Everywhere its effects have permeated all aspects of living in a manner that remains only vaguely and incompletely understood. Like so many other economic and social problems, inflation has been obvious and yet, at best, its causes and effects have only partially been recognized. Public opinion in the United States, until recently, tended to regard inflation as something which existed elsewhere. Horrible examples of inflation were usually far off — in Brazil, in Chile, in Indonesia and Turkey — or closer to home, but still not at home — in France and Britain or immediately postwar Germany. Those in the United States as well as in other countries who recognized the existence of inflation took comfort in the fact that elsewhere the manifestations of inflation were much more virulent and violent: the rise in prices was greater and the injury to the economy more obvious. Moreover, it would prove to be a temporary phenomenon.

Yet inflation and its all-pervasive effects on society have not been the monopoly of any one category of country. Indeed, one of the most thought-provoking aspects of the inflationary phenomenon is that it is found in all kinds of societies, at every stage of economic development, under every variety of government, and within all kinds of political, economic, and social ideologies. We have become accustomed to a great variety of pluralistic societies. We have also become accustomed to seeing these same societies make rapid changes and take sharp turns in their economic and social policies. We have come to take the unexpected for granted. It may even be said that we have come to take disaster for granted. In many countries, continuing inflation has come to be taken for granted.

The people of the United States have finally discovered inflation. Despite the fact that prices increased in nearly every year since the end of World War II, it was not until quite recently, around 1969, that the presence of inflation became a major public issue in the United States. Even then, little was done about it for some time. The awareness of persistent inflation remained vague. The existing inflation is still regarded as a kind of virulent case of temporary inflation, rather than a quite different disease — namely persistent inflation. For many years, even decades, inflation was a subject monopolized by a scattered few: some in the universities, a handful of business and labor leaders, a few governmental officials, and the monetary authorities in the Federal Reserve System.

Within the last couple of years, inflation has become a topic of almost universal interest in the United States. Political leaders, journalists, television commentators now reflect the growing anxieties and concerns of the average person who has been confronted by a rise in prices so rapid and so marked as to be obviously important. Years of persistent but low rates of inflation, 2 percent per year or less, had aroused little widespread interest or concern, perhaps because the rises lacked sufficient drama. Those persistent low rates of inflation were harmful to American society, but not in a manner so obvious that it could not be ignored or dismissed as temporary or unimportant.

By 1969, inflation could no longer remain hidden — and it did not. Cartoonists awoke to the endless ironies and the satirical possibilities of a situation where prices rise rapidly to the discomfort of the many and the pleasures of a few. Virtually from the day of his election, President Nixon and his economic advisers committed themselves to dealing with this problem, taking positions on how it was to be attacked. Finally, in August 1971, their concern culminated in a decision monumental in the economic and political history of the United States: the adoption of wide-ranging governmental price and wage controls in peacetime. That it was done by a political party earnestly dedicated to the principles of noninterference in the operations of the free-enterprise market system only underlined the drama of the event. American history can never again be the same. The "age of dominant government" has been ushered in, and the political contest for control of government takes on greatly heightened significance.

In other industrial countries — Canada, those in Western Europe, and Japan — inflation has been recognized as a problem for a much longer time and by a much larger section of the public. However, for various reasons, each nation has tended to see this problem as something peculiar to itself, having its own unique causes, consequences, and remedies. Perhaps more important, each nation also tended to see the problem as something essentially temporary, one which the next new government, whichever it might be, would tackle with success. As has so often been true, when inflation became widely recognized and publicized as a problem in the United States, other countries began to focus even more attention on the causes of their own inflation. The inability of the United States to deal successfully with its inflation was identified by many as a principal cause of their own inflation, and of their own inability to deal with it.

The less developed countries have had a considerable variety of experience with price inflation. Chronic persistent inflation has reigned in a number of these countries during the entire postwar period. In these countries (if generalizations are possible), many viewed inflation as a "good" thing because they thought that it could help bring about the economic and social transformation we call development. Later, reflecting a growing disenchantment with the possible benefits from inflation, it came to be seen at the least as a nuisance and, by some, as a major handicap to the development process. It was, however, unfortunately also seen as "unavoidable."

That the rate of inflation is higher in one country than in another does not measure the relative damage inflation inflicts on the respective economies and societies. Some economies and some societies are more sensitive to rising prices and costs than others. Social and political conditions, as well as economic, influence their reactions. How long the inflation has already lasted, what its effects have been, whether the public expects it to continue and what the public believes the government can do to change existing trends: these are particularly important factors. Thus, in an industrial country with a very large complex of economic activities, continuous inflation — even at 2 percent per year — may be disruptive. This is particularly so if it follows a period of inflation at a 1 percent rate with the prospect of something higher. By contrast, in agricultural societies, particularly those with sufficient food production, inflation at higher rates may prove more tolerable. In either case, inflation will be less disruptive if people believe the government has the ability to end it in a politically and socially acceptable manner. Or, in countries that have experienced high rates of inflation, a marked decline in the rate represents a major improvement in economic environment and economic management, even though prices continue to rise quite rapidly. Brazil, for example, has reduced its rate of inflation in recent years from about 50 to about 15 percent and this reduction has contributed greatly to Brazil's recent prosperity. But 15 percent per year is still rapid inflation: prices will more than double every four years. Therefore, it is not surprising that people remain highly sensitive to, even skeptical of, the improvement, always looking for signs that the downward trend in prices and costs is being reversed and that the more "normal" situation of rising rates of inflation will reassert itself. Experience has taught people to expect such rising trends, and inflationary expectations die hard.

With price behavior in the 1960s as a guide, the median rate of price increase for a sample of 37 developing countries was about 3.5 percent per annum or a doubling in prices every

20 years. Countries with inflation of this magnitude, or slightly greater, spanned the world: Mexico, Guatemala, and Costa Rica in Central America; Tunisia and the United Arab Republic in North Africa; Ceylon, Pakistan, Thailand, and Malaysia in South and Southeast Asia; and Nigeria in Western Africa. Higher rates of inflation were found throughout the world: Israel, Korea, Trinidad, and Tobago; Indonesia, Kenya, and India. The most rapid inflation occurred mostly in South America: Brazil, Chile, Colombia, Argentina, and Uruguay. These countries experienced price inflation varying from 15 to 50 percent per annum. But the worst case of the 1960s was far from Latin America; it was in Indonesia where inflation ran rampant at over 1000 percent per year. The very fact that the continued strength of price inflation in the major Latin American countries received so much attention obscured the global character of the problem, and the global aspect is what must be recognized.

By the 1960s, rates of inflation in the industrial countries looked very much like the average rate in the developing countries. Indeed, one sign of the new times was the growing acceptance in these countries, however reluctantly by some people, of price increases like 5 percent a year as an "inevitable" feature of modern life — in high income countries as well as low — much as large-scale unemployment had been widely accepted in the late 1930s as "inevitable."

What had been regarded as a national or local problem must now be recognized as world-wide. As in the 1930s, when the economic collapse in the United States merged with economic setback in other countries to form the Great Depression, so we now see national inflations merging into world inflation. If this is true, purely national policies may not be adequate to solve the problem; only some form of international collaboration can provide the framework for successful national policies.

3

Traditional Conceptions
of Inflation

The Role of Rising Prices

There are many different ways of recognizing the presence of inflation — some obvious, some subtle, some even mysterious. The most familiar are the price rises we observe in our daily lives. To most people, prices are seen as they are experienced individually: the price of bread, rice, milk, meat, housing, tuition, bus fares, gasoline, bridge tolls, automobiles, plane fares, shoes, and so forth. Inflation, however, is a rise in virtually all prices simultaneously — *not* a rise in a few while others remain stable or fall.

Prices of individual commodities and services can, and do, change in the normal course of events. A price for an individual commodity or service, in economic practice and theory, results essentially from the interplay of two forces: demand and supply. With a given supply, increases in demand for the product mean, in the first instance, that its price will tend to rise. Producers may respond by increasing output, selling it either at the prevailing higher prices or at lower ones when supply can be augmented sufficiently to meet the increased demand. Conversely, with a given demand, increases in supply tend initially to cause prices to fall, the fall in price tends to cause a reduction in supply. In either case — whether demand or supply is in excess — the market mechanism establishes an "equilibrium" between the two at a single price.

Rises in individual prices, like falls in other individual prices, may well be economically desirable and even essential. Such individual rises are not inflation. This distinction is vital. Too often, needed increases in individual prices are criticized as "inflationary" while, in fact, these very increases may be part of an effective program of bringing down the general level of prices. For example, to encourage the production and import of widely used consumer goods, it may be necessary to curtail sharply the import and production of certain luxury goods. If this is done, the prices of many commodities may well fall but the curtailed commodities will rise in price. The key distinction, of course, is that in a noninflationary environment some individual prices would fall while other individual prices rose as market conditions for individual products changed.

The process of achieving an "equilibrium" price, unless interfered with by other forces, operates in all competitive markets where buyers and sellers meet to trade — from the smallest village to the whole world. All markets are linked to the extent that knowledge of them is available, and that it is possible to respond to that knowledge. As long as the product is transportable, sellers will want to offer their supplies in the market where they know the price to be highest; buyers will seek the product where they know the price to be lowest. But increased supply where prices are high will tend to lower prices, and increased demand where the prices are low will tend to raise them. With perfectly competitive conditions prevailing in all markets, one price would tend to obtain in all. Price differences among markets thus derive essentially from costs of transportation, immobility of goods, and imperfections in knowledge or other impediments such as tariffs on imports or price-fixing arrangements by large firms.

Such rises in prices of particular commodities — in one market or in all — differ from a general rise in prices, when the prices of all goods and services, taken together, increase. This general rise results when demand, again for all goods and services, exceeds what the economy is able to produce. That demand is made "effective" by nominal increases in purchasing power: income and money. In essence, more money "chases" fewer goods; while money or "nominal" income and the amount of money in circulation rise, each dollar buys fewer goods and services, and the purchasing power of money falls. Market forces drive prices up.

The causes of inflation are popularly discussed in terms of "demand-pull" or "cost-push." Demand-pull characterizes inflation when total demand exceeds total supply, creating an "inflationary gap" which is closed as prices rise, all things becoming more expensive and, in money terms, total supply equals total demand. Cost-push characterizes inflation when costs — particularly wages, but also other factors like rent and interest on loans — rise, pushing up the sales price of products to meet these rising costs and still make a tolerable profit: the familiar "wage-price spiral."

The approach to ending inflation differs depending on the

view of its "cause." The demand-pull approach emphasizes reducing the level of general demand to end inflation. The cost-push approach emphasizes keeping wage increases equal to increases in labor productivity; such wage increases need not result in price increases. Neither form of inflation could persist without accompanying inflationary expectations. But such expectations, by the time their presence is recognized, are deep and widespread; they are the evidence that the economy's underlying trend is one of very strong, continuing inflation. Once established, people act on these expectations, heightening demands that strengthen the inflationary spiral.

Inflation has many aspects. Some of them — rising wages and costs of living — are obvious in everyone's experience; others, having been regarded as extraordinary and complex, have been left to the province of highly trained and specialized economists. But with a heightened level of concern, even these aspects have stepped out of the domain of the expert into that of the general public. Columnists can expect to be read and comprehended by a wide audience when they write of inflation's impact on the country's balance of payments or on its exchange rate — matters which only a few years ago were the private domain of the experts. Frequently now, people have decided views about inflation, its causes and effects, and very strong opinions about what government ought or ought not to do about it. At the same time, they still have a gnawing feeling, also frequently revealed, that the subject is so mysterious that it is best left to the expert.

That expert is viewed like some combination of magician and fireman — he should be able to divine means of preventing fires, but, if by chance fires break out, he knows best how to extinguish them. If, in an outburst of zeal and enthusiasm, he floods the entire house ruining it with water instead of fire, his excesses are often only perceived long after the event; the error in judgment is forgotten or never quite understood. Ironically, this worship of the expert grows stronger as people are better or more educated and thus more sensitive of their own limitations, more respectful of those who seemingly know or should know more.

The Mystery of Money

The expert on inflation has a particular advantage, even in a society where technical expertise has quite generally become an object of reverence and awe. He deals with money. There are very few human institutions surrounded with the same aura of the occult as money. Whatever the moral attitude toward money, its great importance is obvious. At the same time, how it comes into being, how it is used, how financial institutions operate generally remain a mystery.

Oddly enough, the economist himself frequently regards money as a "veil" which hides what is really going on in society. People work, start businesses, invest, sell goods, eat, ride cars, buy and live in houses, rent apartments, buy and look at television sets, buy and read newspapers, educate their children (or these days their children's children). These are "real" things. Money only lubricates the machinery that is necessary for the production, distribution, and consumption of these real things. The machinery that money lubricates is the process of exchange, of purchase and sale. Money is the medium of that exchange. It is the common denominator, by which prices of innumerable goods and services can be measured and compared. It makes possible the exchange of the huge variety of goods and services people produce. Money in itself is nothing. It has value only insofar as, and for as long as, people accept it as having value because of its role in the exchange of "real" things. So says the expert! However, the pursuit and acquisition of money is regarded as sensible by most, including the experts, abhorrent and immoral by some, and insane by very few indeed.

Money as a medium of exchange is probably as old as man's organized economic activities. Even at the most primitive level, man used something — cows, oxen, horses, people, seashells, and rocks, copper, tin, silver, and gold — as money. Now we use special kinds of paper printed and issued as currency, usually by a special governmental authority called the central bank, or we use bank checks extensively to exchange bank deposits for goods and services; the latest device is the plastic credit card with a number and a name. Indeed, we seem to be nearing a time when we will need coins only for occasional odd purposes like depositing in parking meters. And cash is something used by the rather "less successful," or the socially unambitious.

For governments, the acquisition and disposal of money is a central activity on which all others depend. Governments regard tax collection as their most important single prerogative. It is the means by which all the other things that modern governments regard as their business are done — enforcing laws; being the largest single employer of the people; building roads, airports, schools, and hospitals; owning real estate; buying and using armaments; subsidizing ship and aircraft building; supplementing the income of farmers, the aged, the unemployed, etc. Closely related to the government's prerogative of taxation is that of borrowing from the public by selling its bonds. Without the ability to tax, the ability to borrow would be greatly weakened since there might then be doubt as to the government's ability to repay its debt.

However, governments' ability to raise money by taxation or by borrowing has, in practice, proved insufficient to meet expenditures. Governments therefore employ a host of other means of increasing their access to money. In earlier centuries they debased coinage, reducing its precious-metal content without reducing its face or monetary value. As a measure of payment or settling debts, this practice was quite the sport of kings. Today, governments do not have to use such limited and crude techniques. Governments now have authority to finance themselves by creating money. This is fiat money, legally declared usable in settlement of any debt. It thus gains public acceptance.

Perhaps most important, fiat money created by the government is multiplied by the operations of the modern banking system. The method is basically very simple. Central banks in most countries — the Federal Reserve System in the United States — usually have the exclusive authority to create money. Essentially this is done by the government's selling its obligations directly to the central bank, exchanging these obligations for deposits, on which the government draws checks to pay its bills. Individuals and firms receive these checks. Most of the checks find their way as deposits to the commercial-bank accounts held by their recipients. Commercial banks are required to place part of any deposit they receive on "reserve" with the central bank. They can then lend — to nearly anyone they please — some or all of the remainder, or make investments such as the purchase of government bonds. These loans and investments also result in deposits, and the deposits are drawn upon. As depositors draw checks, and as these checks are deposited by their recipients in the commercial banks, each bank can increase its lending and investments based on these increased deposits, always adding as required to its reserves with the central bank. As this process works itself out, the commercial-bank system can increase its total loans and investments by a number of times the amount of the original deposit. Thus, the total of all deposits generated by the government's sale of its obligations to the central bank can amount to several times the amount of the initial transaction. In the end, the government has paid its bills and the banking system has greatly expanded its ability to lend to private individuals and firms.

The government can, alternatively, sell its bonds to commercial banks. Payments result in deposits held by the government. From the viewpoint of creating money, it usually matters very little whether the government borrows directly from its central bank or, indirectly, from the commercial banking system.

Money, in this deposit sense, can also be "destroyed," contracting, again multiplicatively, the resources within the banking system. This happens when, for example, the government sells bonds directly to the public, reducing deposit levels in the commercial banks. Or the central bank can increase its minimum reserve requirements, say from 15 percent to 20 percent. This increases the amounts which commercial banks have to deposit with the central bank against their own lending, automatically reducing the volume of credit expansion by the commercial banks. A 15 percent requirement means that a credit expansion of over 6.5 times is possible, while a 20 percent requirement would allow a credit expansion of only about 5 times.

The central bank is the key instrument in money creation. Nevertheless, the central bank remains a government agency; it cannot refuse the government any requested loan. The central bank may have the authority to decide the interest rates which the government must pay, but even this authority to fix rates is subject to government influence. Despite these limitations, it is not surprising that this ability to create money and the institutions which have the prerogative of doing so are regarded everywhere as a responsibility of the highest account, requiring great professional skill and enjoying high social prestige. For people may well not understand why, how, and what the central bank does, but they do sense the great importance of money and money-creating institutions in their daily lives. They do know that at times money seems rather easy to get, while at others it is oppressively absent. The man in the street also knows that, in most cases, his own efforts to obtain money can succeed only if there is some opportunity to pursue some activity that will result in a money income.

The idea that money can be created by government

action, if not fully understood, is nevertheless accepted as a fact of life. But it also illustrates most vividly the view of government as the miracle-doer. If government can miraculously create money, it can do anything. With this psychology, it is a small and comprehensible step to the belief that if the government is unwilling to do something, it is not because it cannot "afford" it, but because it does not believe that something is worth doing.

Because the availability of money is largely determined by the decisions of governments, the final responsibility for its creation rests with those who determine the actions of governments. In all countries these actions are greatly influenced, if not determined, by people — private people. The time has long passed when inflation could be regarded as primarily the concern of the monetary expert. The "money doctor" continues to be needed to diagnose and to prescribe, having analyzed what the effects of different governmental actions are likely to be. Governmental actions are, however, the consequences of judgments or choices made by the patient, not the doctor. Every decision the patient — government — makes affects the amount of money created and what its use will cost. But the patient frequently must decide without full knowledge or regard for the impact on the money supply and the consequences of its use.

Generally governments do recognize that their actions affect the trends in money supply, prices, and wages, and many governments regard such influence, in one way or another, as a primary responsibility. Governments do try to inform the public of their concern with inflation — governments now rarely regard inflation as desirable. However, discussion of inflation is usually designed to appeal to people as "consumers" or to persuade them to exercise restraint in their efforts to increase their incomes as "producers." What it fails to do is to discuss the root causes of inflation, particularly persistent inflation, with its social and political repercussions. Unless he is informed and has ample opportunity to consider these matters, the individual cannot be expected to understand that his political and social views and activities, as well as his economic views and activities, are of paramount importance in explaining inflation and in coping with it.

Demand and Supply: Wages and Prices

It is easy enough to explain why, if people rush to buy goods as in the panic which accompanies threats of war or other disasters, prices will rise sharply. Under such circumstances people use their savings or borrow money or do both to buy what they fear will soon become unavailable or be much more expensive. In this way, money in the economy is used (circulates) more rapidly and its supply may be expanded. What may be less obvious is that when the average citizen supports a political candidate who promises to reduce taxes, he thereby supports a policy that can lead to higher prices and possibly reduce his own standard of living. When he votes for a bond issue to finance airports, schools, roads, or bridges, he may not be aware that in so doing he sets off a chain of events which will ultimately affect the prices he pays for all the things he buys. This applies regardless of what the proposed action may be. In supporting more money for public safety, for schoolteachers, in demanding better utilities like water or electricity or environmental controls, in advocating publicly supported medical care, or in arguing for increasing the level of expenditures on military or foreign assistance, or on a myriad of other things, the actions of individuals as citizens ultimately affect the general level of prices and wages. Of course, the individual does so when he makes personal decisions to spend a certain portion of his own income and save the rest, or when he bargains, individually or collectively, for an increase in his wages. This is easy to see: clearly, a large wage increase is an inducement for the manufacturer to try to obtain a higher price for his product. In a quite analogous manner, the voter plays an active part in major economic decisions affecting both the use of the nation's available resources and the prices to be paid for its goods and services.

In many countries, of course, such policies are not put to the voter in the political process. His influence is then less obvious and more indirect. In any modern society, however, the government requires at least a minimal consent of those governed, and most government activities are of major importance for prices and wages. Thus, even in nondemocratic societies, the attitudes of people toward different public policies and activities are of major importance in determining the course of prices and wages.

Governments have tried to control the level of prices and wages; this is common in socialist countries but much less so in industrial nonsocialist countries. In such cases, the government is acting at the end of the economic process, when its own activities and those of all the other elements in society have already had their effects, creating certain levels of demand for goods and services and determining the supply of goods and services available to meet this demand. Controls are used because prevailing price-wage effects of the demand-supply conditions have become intolerable. The disparity between supply and demand is not only recognized, but is also seen as likely to be eliminated only with unacceptable damage to other national objectives, like low levels of unemployment, high rates of growth, or desired changes in income distribution. Thus, the controls themselves signify a fundamental disequilibrium between demand and supply. They are often adopted in the hope that they will provide the time needed to overcome the supply-demand disparity. That they frequently fail to fulfill these hopes reflects a lack of understanding of why this disparity exists, and how strong the pressures are for it to continue. It is the failure to correct the fundamental causes of the disequilibrium.

In most societies, governments can and do fall, or at least their leadership changes, when the pressures created by their inability to bring about a proper balance between demand and supply become intolerable. These pressures may take the form of very high prices for essential consumption items like food, clothing, and shelter, or, in highly controlled economies, inadequate supplies and low quality. The pressures may take the form of very poor public services, or of wages which prove increasingly less than adequate to cover basic needs. It would be impossible (and unnecessary) to list all the ways in which rising prices affect people's lives. The resultant widespread and deep dissatisfaction undermines the ability to govern. No government can be regarded as strong or stable when the country it governs is experiencing persistent inflation.

It is not surprising that the presence of more and more

inflation, side-by-side with large and persistent unemployment, is today the principal economic concern of countries. It brings into one focus two nightmares — persistent unacceptable unemployment and persistent unacceptable rising prices. What is rather surprising — and indeed frustrating because it means that the problem has become much more serious and much more difficult to deal with successfully — is that the problem has been neglected for so long, even though its presence could be seen for years. A deeper understanding and a much wider awareness of the implications as well as causes of persistent inflation is needed by all; this is so particularly where people have influence on governmental decisions, whether through the political process or through special institutions like trade unions, business associations, or community organizations. Only when this understanding and awareness are achieved will people be able to choose intelligently among public policies.

The question which now confronts people everywhere is how important is it to stop the chronic rise in prices found in most countries which we call persistent inflation, and how can it be stopped effectively with least social cost? To make these judgments people need to know something about how persistent inflation arises, how it manifests itself, what its major effects are, and what might be done. There are, in my view, very few questions which have more significance for each individual, his family, his community, his nation, and the world.

4

Setting the Stage
for Persistent Inflation

Prejudice versus Fact

The legacy of past differences of views on how best to
manage the economy, particularly on the responsibilities and
role of government and on the efficiency and equity of a free-
enterprise economy operating through the market mechanism, has affected attitudes on inflation. Attitudes become
tangled with political antagonisms and biases.

To be against inflation is often identified with being politically conservative and against social and economic progress:
against achieving and maintaining high levels of employment, against social security, free medical care, and other
benefits of the twentieth-century version of the welfare
state. Opposition to inflation is regarded as reflecting a cruel
indifference to poverty and social discrimination, as uphold-
ing the worst features of the status quo and opposing social
mobility and new economic opportunities. It is criticized as
indifference to glaring inequalities in income distribution.
These views prevail because the seriousness of the damage
caused by persistent inflation is even as yet not appreciated,
nor is the depth of the problem sufficiently understood.

The "liberal" for his part tends to suspect the conservative's antagonism toward inflation. Is the latter's antagonism really directed at full employment, higher wages, and strong trade unions? Does his opposition to inflation really hide more deeply felt social biases and political prejudices? At the same time, the political conservative often espouses anti-inflation or stabilization policies for very different reasons. He is displeased by government's readiness to greatly extend its area of responsibility: expanded government, he believes, threatens personal liberty, initiative, and self-reliance. The liberal finds himself at least tolerating government policies which, by resulting in inflation, deeply hurt the poorest and least protected sectors of society as well as others.

Consideration of inflation has indeed become confused, muddled, and befuddled. Nevertheless, the public must, in the final analysis, judge and evaluate economic and social conditions and trends. Each citizen makes deliberate choices — by voting as part of the national political jury or by otherwise indicating his preferences; his choices support or oppose policies that will maintain or change existing conditions. While he is making these choices, incomprehensible statistics, charts, analyses, and government "white papers" all bombard him. No wonder he either follows a leader, or votes his prejudices.

The Legacy of Depression and War: the All-Importance of Full Employment Policy

Before turning to persistent inflation as it now presents itself, we must unravel the peculiar tangle of political and social biases that have colored much of the thinking, writing, and action in this field, particularly in the immediate postwar era when public policy decisions paved the way for the advent of persistent inflation around the world. The Great Depression of the 1930s profoundly affected attitudes on all economic, social, and political questions of people who lived through it. The leadership of the world in all spheres of human activity is still largely exercised by people so affected. During the depression, unemployment rates of 15 percent and more were widespread. Worse, these endured for many years. Arguments about the precise figures will go on forever, but it cannot be far wrong to say that the United States alone had between 10 to 15 million unemployed in the 1930s or about 20 to 25 percent of the labor force, and possibly more. The unbelievable waste — tens of millions of people throughout the world eager and able to work but unable to secure employment despite the fact that plants and equipment everywhere stood idle — was obvious.

Less obvious, but at least equally important, was the resulting widespread social misery in terms of disrupted family relations, frustrated expectations, vanishing hopes; there was disillusionment with existing economic and political systems; many were eager to see radical changes; others lost confidence in the ability of democratic institutions to survive. The political upheavals seen then, and still seen by many, as the primary cause of the most destructive war in history, grew out of the depression: the rise of Nazism, coupled with the widespread fear of communism; the rise of economic nationalism and "beggar-thy-neighbor" foreign trading policies, which desperately and unsuccessfully tried to improve domestic conditions even by actions deliberately harmful to

other nations in similarly deplorable conditions; the collapse
of prices of raw material, like rubber and coffee, which hit
hardest the poorest countries; the widespread defaults on
international financial obligations; the breakdown of historic,
political, and military alliances, and the resulting impotence
of all significant attempts to achieve some international
order; the repeated outbreaks of war in China, Ethiopia, and
Spain, and so forth. Newspaper headlines all over the world
dramatically announced the collapse of nations and the futil-
ity of their efforts to stem the rising flood of economic
disaster and social disorder. All seemed linked to one fact —
large-scale continuous unemployment. In the United States
and elsewhere that fact remained indelibly imprinted in the
cultural memory: it was the sin never to be repeated.

But together with unemployment in the 1930s came a
sharp fall in prices. In consequence, price declines were
regarded as portents of continued depression, while price
increases were heralded, often wrongly, as portents of improvement. They were viewed as the mechanism for inducing more investment and thus creating more jobs, setting in
motion the sought-after upswing in the business cycle. Employed people might suffer somewhat from the fall in the
purchasing power of their wages as prices rose, but this was
obviously a small cost when compared to the benefits of
putting millions of people back to work, activating idle
plants.

Furthermore, the lasting impression of the persistence of
unemployment was greatly enhanced by the failure to cure
the problem by peacetime measures. Large government expenditures and even budgetary deficits — hitherto a sign of

financial difficulties, if not mismanagement — were widely tolerated to help trigger the desired recovery. But the measures taken did not prove adequate. It took preparation for war, and war itself to overcome the Great Depression. In Germany, prolonged severe depression had made possible the accession of the Nazis to power; their policy was — to echo a much-publicized Nazi slogan — guns, not butter. Nazi Germany eliminated unemployment by preparing for war.

Thus it is understandable why "full employment" was adopted as a national target by the United Kingdom, the United States, and others, and why to this day, memories of the Great Depression, though growing dimmer and pushed by some into the subconscious, remain a most potent force in economic and social thinking. The avoidance of another Great Depression became the number one economic priority of the postwar world.

The intellectual basis for such thinking was being laid even as the depression persisted. Its best known expression is in the writings of John Maynard Keynes, particularly his most famous work, *The General Theory of Employment, Interest and Money*. But many of the ideas in it had, in fact, evolved over a number of years, especially within the oral tradition at Cambridge University in England.

To those at Cambridge — and to some elsewhere — the accepted doctrine of economic theory stood sharply at variance with the economic phenomena they observed. Doctrine held that "supply creates its own demand." The income received by laborers in their various activities would purchase the output produced and, with only short-lived, temporary setbacks, would provide full employment. For many decades this picture of the world had approximated reality. Yet, from 1926 in the United Kingdom, unemployment had been at record levels, while plants remained idle. Economic doctrine held that inadequate demand could arise, but only as a local, temporary phenomenon. Yet large scale unemployment and low private investment plagued the whole country. Moreover, it appeared that the economy had attained a lasting equilibrium at these low levels of activity and high levels of unemployment. Doctrine, by contrast, asserted that equilibrium could occur only at full employment.

Keynes's *General Theory* offered an explanation. Expectations of future profit induce investment. Investors borrow to augment their activity, and are normally willing to do so as long as their expected rate of return covers their "costs," including not only payments for labor, rent, and supplies, but also for interest on borrowed funds and a profit sufficient to make the investment worthwhile. If it cost less to borrow, they could invest more. Hence there is a clear role for monetary policy: by altering monetary policy — reducing interest rates and increasing credit availability — the monetary authorities should be able to stimulate investment. But, Keynes said, when profit expectations are extremely low, even at low interest rates, investors might prefer to hold liquid assets, cash, rather than increase activity at all. Under these circumstances — the much-debated Keynesian "liquidity trap" — monetary policy would prove totally ineffective. An economy could then attain equilibrium with low levels of supply balancing low levels of demand, even though unemployment of significant magnitude prevailed.

Fiscal policy — tax reductions or government expenditure increases — could, however, act effectively to stir the economy where monetary policy could not. Government expenditure could supplement inadequate private investment; it would stimulate the economy in a way directly analogous to increased private investment. The consequences would be increased employment, increased income, increased demand — both for production and consumption goods. The economy could approach a new equilibrium, where employment, if not full, was greatly increased.

This sort of reasoning would, by the late 1940s, be more widely known. How influential these ideas of the "new economics" were in formulating governments' policies during the depression is still debated. At best, they were tried. But they conflicted with strongly held traditional views that government expenditures ought to be minimized, particularly during depressions when tax revenues declined, and that economies would recover more quickly and with better results if the market mechanism was allowed to operate free of governmental interference. Large increases in fiscal expenditures to stimulate the economy were regarded as governmental interference in the market mechanism. "Anticyclical" measures, particularly the advocated increases in government expenditures and consequent acceptances of large budgetary deficits, were tried only halfheartedly. But World War II intervened, and inadvertently provided an example of the power of high levels of government activity to stimulate economies.

The Successful Wartime Role of Big Government

Contrasting with the frustrations and failures of the Great Depression and with the horror of World War II was the simple fact that the war economies eliminated unemployment. War had demonstrated what had been argued with only partial success: governments could do away with unemployment. Substitute civilian activities for military, and the same trick would work in peacetime. Unemployed people were again seen as potential assets, not liabilities, to the economy and to society, as long as there were tools for them to work with.

Demand could be created for the products of a much larger, fully employed labor force. In the United States, satisfactory consumption standards were maintained while huge numbers were in the armed forces or producing war material. This performance was made possible by the absorption of over ten million unemployed. Due credit must, of course, be given to the women who became welders instead of homemakers, and to the almost unbelievable increase in labor efficiency and productivity, both in the factory and on the farm. Production, we had learned, could be planned to leap upward, quickly and with certainty, at the beckoning of the government.

Another legacy of the war was a marked change in peacetime attitudes toward governmental expenditures and taxation: toward budget deficits, national debt, and interest rates. Huge deficits, massive increases in national debt, and fixed low-interest rates — which cut the costs not only of that debt but also of private investment and consumption — were instruments of the wartime economy. Wartime taxation and government expenditures were so huge that both could fall after the war and still remain extremely high by peacetime standards. But the war was won and unemployment abolished!

Large government expenditures were a familiar part of wartime experience. What was new was the conviction that these wartime fiscal policies proved the validity of the argument that large-scale government expenditures could successfully cope with the peacetime problems of large-scale continuing unemployment and economic stagnation. Clearly, to favor continuing such fiscal practices was to help prevent their re-emergence.

During the war the demand for goods exceeded supply, creating the then widely publicized "inflationary gap." Prices had been kept from rising by extensive price, wage, and production controls. "Suppressed" inflation replaced "open" inflation. "Open" inflation would have meant allowing prices and wages to rise sharply in response to the large increases in demand — for war materials as well as for civilian consumption and investment goods as incomes and profits rose — while supplies of labor and raw materials needed for production and for plant and equipment became increasingly short.

To preclude this process, war economies were imposed. Prices and wages were held down, "suppressed." The government, instead of the market mechanism, took responsibility not only for the general levels of prices and wages, but also for specific prices and wages, and thus for the whole pattern of relative prices and wages. The market mechanism no longer reflected consumer demands and business decisions in response to them. Goods and services were still exchanged for money. It looked like a "market economy." The vehicles of the market economy, like banks, privately owned factories, farms, trucks, stores, and gasoline stations were used. But the economic function of prices, to reflect changes in conditions of demand for and supply of goods and services, and to provide the signals for adjusting consumption, production and trade to shifts in demand and supply were taken over by the government. Instead of millions of economic units — mostly private individuals and firms — ruling the markets, it was now largely ruled by public officials with the advice of consultants from the private world.

Controlled prices reflected calculated expected costs, including wages, and provided for reasonable profit margins. They were not set irresponsibly, or stupidly, or in ignorance of conditions in the economy or particular industries. By and large, they were carefully considered and well adhered to. But the pattern of production and consumption reflected wartime needs, not to be judged by peacetime standards. The controls did not bring demand and supply into equilibrium by the shifting of relative prices and wages; demand for consumption goods was particularly suppressed and remained largely unmet, so individuals had little alternative but to accumulate large savings. Consumer and producer goods were "rationed" by detailed complex government regulations; these were administered at the consumer level principally by storekeepers and gasoline station attendants who acted as unpaid government officials. Leaving aside the widespread black markets that not surprisingly arose, keeping down prices of rationed goods frequently required government payments or subsidies to producers to assure that necessary production continued while prices were kept down. The United States and other war economies did use incentives (wages, profits, dividends, etc.), but the government, not consumers and producers, dominated. The system of controls worked reasonably well because of public acceptance. War needs were paramount and, in any case, all expected that these controls were temporary and would be eliminated after the war.

Consumption was held back while incomes rose. People were encouraged to save instead of consume. Savings were attractive not only because they were patriotic, but they were expected to maintain their purchasing power in the postwar period. The resultant increased savings — in war bonds, bank deposits, and other liquid assets — would create the basis for a huge and sudden increase in demand after the war. Moreover, because of price controls, the purchasing power of these savings was, at least for the moment, not being eroded by inflation.

That the accumulation of purchasing power would be a major factor in the immediate postwar period was recognized. But its inflationary consequences were not — and probably could not have been — fully predicted. Again, any risk taken was, quite correctly, a small price to pay for winning the war. And there were many who did not see risk but, rather, advantage in the large accumulation of purchasing power. Because the market economies of the United States, Britain, and elsewhere had not solved the problem in peacetime of large-scale unemployment, the fear and expectation that peace would bring back the depressed conditions of the 1930s was widespread. The unprecedented backlog of consumer demand, coupled with the large amounts of savings accumulated during the war, were thus welcomed; they would provide offsets to the depressing conditions of "normalcy" which many expected to return after the war. Prices might rise as a result of this pent-up demand, but the increases were expected to be moderate and temporary. On the contrary, the stage was, in fact, being set for persistent, not temporary, peacetime inflation of major, not moderate, proportions.

5

The New World of 1945

The Welfare State

Less directly attributable to the war, but nevertheless at least accelerated in time by the social attitudes which the war strengthened, was the final acceptance of the welfare state. In fact, the welfare state had been developing for a hundred years and social and economic historians can surely find earlier analogies if not roots. The widely held viewpoint in the mid-1940s which might well be called Beveridgism — the moral concern with poverty accompanying industrialization that was greatly influenced by the pioneering works and activities of the English statesman Sir William Beveridge in the field of social legislation — had taken hold in various countries, including the United Kingdom and the United States. And countries like Australia, Germany, Sweden, and New Zealand had already gone very far in making the welfare state a reality.

In many respects the acceptance of the welfare state was quite similar to the acceptance of governmental responsibility for avoiding prolonged and severe depression. But the welfare state not only has different historical roots — largely humanitarian concern with the poor, needy, and chronically unemployed — it enhances the role of government beyond the employment responsibility. It encompasses all people — unemployable or not — and involves manifold aspects of their lives. For example, the concepts that individuals should not have to be concerned about hardships during old age, or lack medical facilities, or be denied opportunities for higher education because of inadequate income were added to that of protection from economic hardships during unwanted unemployment. These became accepted political and social conventions and soon after the end of World War II were enacted into laws of countries everywhere.

Such concepts were embodied in legislation or included in constitutions irrespective of the capacity of the governments to fulfill the obligations they implied. Even in developing countries, these social concepts were transformed into governmental obligations. Countries did, and still do, differ in the scope and generosity of welfare assistance and most, in practice, did not fulfill their declared obligations. In particular countries, certain areas of social security remained uncovered and certain sectors of the population received the benefits later than others. Nonetheless, the actuality or the goal of economic and social security now became an obligation universally accepted in principle by governments and very widely applied in practice.

The transformation in social, political, and cultural value systems implied the need to achieve an adequate economic foundation, which in many countries did not exist. Full employment and economic growth at rates achieved in the past were, however, all that was thought required to enable these social benefits to be generalized throughout the population. The implications for the functioning and management of societies were glossed over in an eagerness to participate in this new stage in the evolution of man's sense of responsibility to others, and in the fear of the political consequences of any seeming foot-dragging. Acceptance of social security, in all its forms, was the flowering of the Victorian spirit — optimistic and morally concerned — united with the reinforced confidence in the miraculous powers of government consequent upon the war experience and buttressed by Keynesian economic reasoning.

Everywhere political groups and leaders pledged allegiance to these welfare goals. In nearly all countries the goals became so firmly part of accepted political customs and activities that no other national priorities, except full employment and national defense, have competed for first place. Commitments to full employment and welfare gained an authority which only free trade and the self-regulated market mechanism had had in the late nineteenth and early twentieth centuries.

Reconstruction and the Creation of Prosperity

Perhaps the most obvious need at the end of World War II was to reconstruct much of the industrial world. The United States, Canada, the United Kingdom, the U.S.S.R., Belgium, the Netherlands, Germany, France, Japan, Italy, Norway, Denmark, Austria, and Czechoslovakia — these were most of the industrial nations in 1939, and were all involved in the war. Only Sweden and Switzerland among the industrialized nations had not been directly involved. Of those involved, only the United States and Canada had not suffered major war damage, whether by direct destruction or poor maintenance of plant and equipment.

War had destroyed much of industry in Europe and Japan. The violence of World War II was so shocking as to leave people numb. Refuge was sought, and found, in bloodless statistics, and consolation in the thought of how much worse the world would have been if the war had been lost. Some went so far as to propose that, in rebuilding Germany, it be constrained to a much less industrialized economy because German industry had provided the means for the nearly successful Nazi war machine. Even leaving aside the devastating impact on people and interpersonal relations, the economic effects brought European civilization close to oblivion. The destruction had to be speedily repaired. Humanitarian concerns as well as fear of political upheavals reinforced this conviction.

At first nearly all seemed gone; but survey missions to Germany and to Japan revealed that something remained even there. The magnitude of investment that would be needed to re-create industrial capacity and put labor back to work was unknown in 1945. Obviously, however, it would take on gigantic dimensions. Roads, bridges, railroads, schools, hospitals, churches, museums, dams, utilities, public buildings — much of the infrastructure built over centuries — had been destroyed or damaged. Fortunately, despite the unprecedented magnitude of the task, the war experience had given people the confidence that government-led reconstruction could, in a few years, create a new industrial structure in Europe and Japan, provide the needed infrastructure, and put people back to work. That confidence underlaid the decision, in 1947, to create the Marshall Plan.

The focal point of the Marshall Plan was the quickest possible reconstruction; its success was read as a victory for government-led reconstruction. It was a great success, economically as well as politically. Western Europe and Japan not only speedily reached prewar production levels, but very soon exceeded them. Unemployment was virtually eliminated and rates of growth higher than prewar rates were achieved and maintained. Sustained unprecedented prosperity followed reconstruction. Special problems, like housing, continued, but new technologies greatly accelerated the solution of many problems, and, more generally, stimulated economies. The success of the Marshall Plan strengthened the conviction, itself confirmed during the war, that governments could avoid a return to the abhorred depression of the 1930s.

Even the United States and Canada had needed time, though few anticipated how little, to convert to a peacetime economy: to retool industry, to absorb a labor force swelled by former members of the armed forces and to replace obsolescent plants, railways, etc. All this was done in a manner which took advantage of the technologies developed to win the war. War-encouraged technologies, once applied to peacetime activities, would revolutionize peacetime production and distribution. History had repeatedly taught that wartime technology could be translated to peacetime uses; indeed, some historians and sociologists saw periods of arma-

ment build-up and war as the great periods of accelerated
innovation and invention.

What was not seen was that though the United States and
Canada greatly increased their productive capacities, the
magnitude of the postwar tasks and demands would inevitably strain even these economies. Excessive demand, rather
than the feared inadequate demands, would become the more
normal state of affairs. Obsolescence, due in part to the inevitable neglect of plant and equipment under the pressures of
war demand, and the development of new technologies combined to increase the demands on the immediate postwar
economies. Obsolescence added to the need for capital.
New technologies not only increased and broadened the
capacity to produce, but also increased demand for new
capital as well as the commodities produced. Many of the
techniques developed in Great Britain, Germany, the United
States, and the U.S.S.R. had obvious peacetime uses: new
chemicals would eliminate dread diseases like malaria and
pneumonia; there were expanded radio communication, com-
puters, television, other electronic advantages, large and long-
range airplanes, and the release of nuclear energy.

The Onset of Consumerism

Despite the world-wide destruction, an evident, if paradox-
ical, consequence of the war was greatly heightened expectations about the future, particularly for material well-being.
Early in the twentieth century, the Victorian confidence in
continuing progress had been given an American twist. The
century had been heralded as the era of rising expectations.

World War I had accelerated the industrialization of the American economy. The 1920s saw, for many, the realization of the "American Dream": plentiful food, adequate clothing, greatly improved housing, automobiles, indoor plumbing, stoves, refrigerators, and electricity everywhere, free education through the university. Country lanes were turning into fast turnpikes and motorways, increasingly available to larger and larger numbers. Thus began the Americanization of America, which laid the basis for the Americanization of the world. Nor was the dream ended by the Great Depression.

It remained only for the economic prodigies performed during the war to prove again the practicality of the American Dream. But now it was to encompass all people everywhere, in all countries, in cities and on the farms. The United States in World War II had mounted the greatest military effort in history and had still provided a rising living standard for its people. The dream became more vivid, more richly colored. It meant new definitions for acceptable living standards and for poverty. During World War II, automobile dealers had amassed a backlog of large volumes of orders for new cars; similar was the demand for new housing, refrigerators, and other consumer durables. At the same time, new concepts of quality and variety in nutrition, clothing, and personal appearance arose (cosmetics production was becoming a multibillion-dollar-a-year industry). With steady employment and liberal use of increasingly available consumer purchasing credit, such purchases were to become part of the ordinary American's way of life. The barefoot boy was no longer the "model" of American youth; he became a historical legend, as did the self-educated, self-made, or even nearly illiterate president of a firm, or the poor white or black farmer living in a "romantic" one-room shack. America's new concept of what every American ought to have by way of material well-being made poverty socially intolerable and politically unacceptable. It was to be eliminated as soon as possible, with repeated apologies for failures or delays in doing so. The concept of the era of rising expectations was thus transformed by the war from that of stately, modest steps, however steady, reflecting the caution as well as the optimism of the Victorian age, into that of giant strides and leaps in improving material well-being. The United States and others later had taken the path that led to modern-day "consumerism."

Emphasis on consumer goods as such may, however, give a lopsided impression of the American Dream as it emerged from World War II. It also contained aesthetic and spiritual elements — more and better education, more beautiful buildings, more art galleries, more creative art, more music. The United States armed forces had seen the world, and the GI Bill of Rights, designed to make possible a better way of life, was the consummation of the American belief in the value of universal education. These standards, too, became part of the Americanization of world consumption standards. Everywhere they took root, the exclusiveness of higher education was challenged and significant democratization in education resulted. In education, as in many other things, this Americanization meant the absorption of many ideas and practices which had originated and flourished earlier in other countries. The American contribution was to envisage those benefits as available and usable by people everywhere.

The Americanization of European consumption had begun before World War II, but now Americanization would mean consumption at new levels, much higher than in the prewar United States. Europe and Japan as well as North America are still reeling under this impact of changes in consumption expectations. In economically underdeveloped areas, American consumption standards had become known to many, but very few could attain them. For the large remainder they represented a source of embittering frustration. Before the war in these countries, complaints of widespread poverty failed to evoke from governments even a promise of quick change. After World War II, governments could not survive, nor could opposition parties come into power unless they promised rapid, general, and major improvements in material well-being.

Mass media spread these ideas nearly instantaneously. Newspapers, magazines, cinema, radio, and television made all vivid and real. Advertising, already integral to the American economic system, was copied everywhere. Purchasing on credit, also already well-known, was likewise widely copied. Thus, consumer tastes as well as production technologies were spread world-wide with amazing rapidity — a key factor in creating the world-wide phenomenon of persistent inflation.

Realization that the American Dream would, in turn, create serious political, social, and economic problems was at best only dim. The aim was to make everyone affluent. The hangovers or hang-ups such affluence would create had to be learned from painful experience: from persistent inflation to increased hardships for large sections of the population, to burning cities, increased crime, and drug addiction. The seeds of the complacent 1950s, the troubled 1960s and the still alienated 1970s are to be found in the conditions and attitudes which came out of World War II.

The New World Setting

The stage was set for a new period in world economic history. For the industrialized countries of Europe, North America, Japan, Australia, and New Zealand, it would be one of exceptionally high national growth, low levels of unemployment, mini-recessions compared with the 1930s experience, and of unprecedented expansion in world trade. But these would come together with equally unprecedented effects. For the developing countries, there would also be relatively rapid growth as governments took the lead in accelerating social and economic development. But widespread poverty would continue, population would explode with increasing and often massive unemployment and great disparities in the distribution of income. With this would come chronic social and political instability, exacerbating the already great difficulties of constructing the private and public institutions needed to carry on viable economies and societies. It would be a period of rapid evolution toward a world economy, instead of national (or imperial) economies, each experiencing fairly separated economic trends. Moreover, government, management, and labor would interact in a manner which substantially altered the fundamental character of the market economy. Rising expectations of people everywhere would become a tidal wave. Previous distinctions like the materialistic West and the nonmaterialistic East would prove anachronistic. Material well-being would be the target of every society and marked differences in material well-being among countries and within countries were to be sharply criticized and deliberate government measures taken to narrow them. Unexpected results — the population explosion, with world population rising from 2.5 billion in 1950 to 4 billion in 1970, and environmental pollution — were to be among the products. But they were first to be viewed as the products of success, not failure.

The stage was also set for chronic and marked inflation. The cat was in the bag. The new economic and social conditions, despite (some may say because of) the increased role of government, would result in a sustained demand for goods and services that would tend to outrun supply nearly everywhere even though output was rising steadily. New demands would quickly substitute for older ones as soon as they were satisfied. Chronic scarcity amidst rising affluence was the seeming paradox. The gains from increased productive capacity were soon outrun by greater increases in demand.

The changed expectations that emerged from World War II were to be sought in a markedly different economic, social, and political framework. The framework itself greatly affected not only the ability of societies to fulfill these expectations, but the way in which the efforts themselves would, in turn, affect societies. Among the important changes in this framework were the new positions, roles, and attitudes of labor, management, and government.

Organized labor, in World War II, had become "respectable" while management became public-relations minded, particularly as management was increasingly divorced from ownership, and less and less eager to experience industrial strife. Fierce and violent labor disputes were still to be experienced; but these were increasingly to be exceptional and sporadic. In the United States, nonagricultural employment was to increase by over 50 percent between 1950 and 1970, with a corresponding increase in total number of man-days worked each year. During this same period the absolute number of workers involved in work stoppages remained about the same; this amounted to about 5 percent of the labor force in 1950, but declined to only about 3 percent in 1970. Similar declines were recorded in the relative number of idle man-days resulting from work stoppages. Both management and labor of the larger firms continued to be, or at least to sound worried about rises in prices and wages — management with wages, and labor with prices. Neither, however, got too excited when it became clear that for their industries and firms the prevailing price trends meant that the final-price increases accommodated both. Both became strong supporters of policies designed to maintain high levels of employment, even though it meant modifying their strong opposition to government budget deficits. Industry accepted continued high levels of taxation, despite the fact that personal and corporate income taxes were many times higher than before the war. Even employees — most of whom had never paid income taxes at all — now regarded such high levels of taxation as normal.

Perhaps most important, industry and labor accepted the new paternalistic or leadership role of government. Out of the war experience, a new and powerful triumvirate arose: Big Government, Big Business, and Big Labor.

With government emerging as the largest single buyer of goods and services, labor and management quickly learned that often they need not dispute wages; whatever wages were agreed within the governmental guidelines mattered little to the producer fulfilling a government contract. The largest consumer, the government, was ready to cover all costs and provide a reasonable profit margin. Government could deliver on prosperity and that was all-important, whatever ideologies might be professed by individual managers or trade-union leaders. Moreover, government was not necessarily either prolabor or promanagement, as many had contended in the decades before World War II. Government was subject to simultaneous pressures from all groups. Different parties at different times leaned more toward labor or more toward management. But opposing winds kept government from leaning too much in one direction for any length of time. Over time, government tended to act to avoid disturbing markedly the distribution of income between industry and labor. In many countries, governments consistently were partial to farmers. This was "politics," to be tolerated by management and labor alike — as long as industrial wage income and profits continued to rise.

Expanded roles for government and the new importance of huge industrial firms and complexes paralleled by powerful trade unions created a new environment for the operation of the market price system. Even before World War II, competition in a number of industries had diminished. In many cases, a few large firms supplied the market; they could, if they desired, "administer" prices rather than allow the market to determine them. Antitrust legislation, particularly in the United States, had, at most, slowed down this process. In continental Europe, operation of business through large cartels had long been commonplace and was still encouraged. The free enterprise system was to continue to be profit- and market-oriented. The market mechanism would still play a major role in economic activity. But the competitive market mechanism as it existed in earlier years — very likely never as completely competitive as many assumed — was probably gone for the predictable future, if not forever.

The new postwar market mechanism with its greatly reduced competitive forces proved inflation-prone. Demand — of consumers, industry, and governments — was normally high. Often, moreover, its level was little affected by increases in prices. And, given fiscal and monetary policies designed to finance high levels of demand, the new market mechanism was one much more likely to adjust to changing conditions by raising prices and wages than by holding them down. Indeed, in time the new market system would be regarded as making inflation tolerable, inevitable, or even desirable. The pattern was set for industrial relations in which the ability to pass on cost increases to the buyer of output was a major influence. Immediate postwar needs and demands were to be worked out within this greatly altered and inflation-prone market mechanism.

Destiny seemed to be determined that the decades after World War II should be ones of persistent rising prices. In addition to the expansionary factors already described, additional forces emerged soon after World War II which strongly reinforced that direction. One was the Cold War; another, the emergence of new nations.

The Cold War

Because of the Cold War, military expenditures in the United States, the United Kingdom, France, and the U.S.S.R. remained high, whether measured as proportions of the gross national product or of the total budget. It meant that, even aside from other strong forces making for increased governmental expenditures, levels of government expenditures and taxation similar to those that prevailed in peacetime before World War II could not return.

It was not obvious in the late 1940s that the military expenditures would give rise to what President Eisenhower called the military-industrial complex. But the probable economic consequences were — or perhaps should have been — evident from what countries had experienced in the "hot" war. Large defense expenditures would increase income throughout the economy, without corresponding products and services being produced; military expenditures are inherently unproductive. Government would be a "consumer" that did not argue about price because it wanted to, or believed it had to, maintain industrial peace in the armaments industries to have their fullest cooperation. It would encourage investments, making manufacturers optimistic about the availability of markets. It would spend very large sums on research and development to continue to accelerate technological change and this would induce even more rapid obsolescence and increased demand for new investments. Government would diminish the labor force by retaining a large armed force. Also in other ways it would help create bottlenecks in productive capacity or in specialized manpower availability. In any environment, high levels of military expenditures cannot but contribute to inflation.

During the war it had been clearly understood that increased military expenditures meant a corresponding reduction of civilian expenditures enforced by governmental controls. With the war's end, however, there was a rapid return to a civilian mentality in which military expenditures were again recognized as a major factor determining national economic conditions, but they were not seen as alternatives to private consumption. Indeed, by helping to achieve full employment, they might even be regarded as making feasible higher consumption by stimulating higher levels of total output. A 100 percent employed economy could devote 5 to 10 percent of its output to defense and, so the argument ran, still have more cushion for peacetime purposes than an 80 to 85 percent employed economy.

This attitude was not unrealistic when peacetime military budgets were relatively small, even in the relatively important military powers like Great Britain, France, the Soviet Union, and the United States. But the Cold War was not "peacetime" — either in concept, or in the size of armament expenditures. Economically, the situation was more like one of major war. Military expenditures were to remain the biggest single item in the national budgets of a number of the largest — economically speaking — countries in the world. The impact of this Cold War level of expenditures on economies and their societies was, moreover, much larger and more profound than the percentages of total output devoted to armaments or other defense purposes. Leaving aside the social and political dimensions, these armament expenditures came on top of demands already large enough to make full employment conditions possible, while reducing the output of civilian goods and services. As in so many other ways, many early postwar analyses underestimated the inflationary pressures which would arise from these military expenditures.

Emerging Nations

Another important expansionary force that emerged in the early postwar period was the formation of new nations. The transformation of the British Empire into the British Commonwealth had begun before the war. The Statute of Westminster of 1931 had envisaged a gradual process of transformation from empire to a commonwealth of independent nations. Egypt was independent. The independence of the Philippines was scheduled to take place in 1946. Yet most of the "colonial" world, which encompassed a majority of the world's people, had not yet become fully independent by the outbreak of World War II. The direction of change was clear, but its pace was slow and cautious.

During World War II, it had become evident that that pace would quicken. New nations would emerge quickly in the postwar world. Even at the international conferences during the war, India and the Philippines had played important independent roles. China and India, particularly, were expected to be significant in postwar international affairs.

The future of certain areas, like the then Netherlands Indies which were to become Indonesia, was still not clear. It was surmised that some form of self-government, if not formal independence, would emerge. That this process of accelerated nation building was going to be costly, even with a minimal definition of the role of government, was evident. However, the rapidity and extensiveness with which new nations burst forth in the 1950s and into the 1960s was not generally foreseen. By the early 1960s nearly all of the people of the world would live in independent, sovereign nation-states.

For a new nation, dignity and self-pride are even more important than for the well-established nations. Colonial governments left behind their buildings, but only few would give pride to the new national consciousness. Some, like India, would inherit great capital cities like New Delhi, but these were exceptional. Others, like Pakistan, were destined to have three capitals in twenty years, seeking in vain for a capital that would serve to unite a nation made up of two distinct geographic areas separated by nearly a thousand miles of India. And as this is written, Pakistan has broken into two. A new nation, Bangladesh, with a new national capital, Dacca, is being formed and beginning the endless journey of a new nation. Moreover, there were older nations like those in Latin America which had achieved political independence many years before, but had not attained what they regarded as their proper status and recognition in the world. These experienced the same emotions as the newly independent nations.

However, the benefits and the costs of the race — against

time and in competition with other new nations — for visible national dignity and pride were neither understood nor
appreciated. Self-government or independence would require services in addition to those provided under colonial
rule: new public buildings, if not new capital cities, to reflect
the strong young national pride; new hospitals designed for
people urgently needing, demanding, and expecting the
benefits of modern medicine; new schools to educate the
illiterate who were now full-fledged citizens; independent
armed forces and, frequently, national airlines however
uneconomic; embassies, and a much larger civil service with
as few "foreigners" as possible; new roads that would facilitate military and civilian transport but would also help bring
about or reflect the new sense of national unity and destiny.
Institutions in the United States, Britain, and France provided the principal models for the new nations. The political
leaders and government personnel of the newly independent
nations had, frequently, been trained there; foreign advisers
often came from there.

To many, all this seemed and still seems wasteful and
irresponsible, well beyond the means of those new countries.
With the exception of the producers of minerals (e.g., oil
and copper), most shared a common inheritance of widespread poverty and very limited resources. Many were in
difficult-to-develop tropical areas. Even the United States
did not fully appreciate these sentiments though its nationhood was relatively new and in 1945 many were alive who
had seen new states in the Union build stately governor's
mansions, buildings for their state legislatures modeled on the
national capitol, and university campuses reflective of com-

munity pride. As for Englishmen and Frenchmen, why didn't many more understand the spirit which had built Notre Dame and Versailles, or Westminster and Whitehall? Was the building of Brasilia so different? St. Peter's in Rome had strained the resources of the Church to the breaking point. Some of the newer countries, smarting from years of colonial rule and eager to assert themselves, rushed to demonstrate their pride in nationhood. Who is to say how history will judge these expenditures so many now scorn? Perhaps they will be accepted as an inevitable part of the process of state-making that left behind lasting structures of use and aesthetic value to the community. We will not know the answer, at least until we know whether the new nations will use their pride in statehood as the instrument to create the national will and ability to deal more effectively with their deep social, economic, and political problems.

More important, both from a general economic viewpoint and for understanding the near universality of persistent inflationary pressures, these countries took on the same expanded and expanding role of government found in the industrialized nations — the same concepts of welfare, security, material well-being, the same desire for universality of education. Indeed, they would, in a sense, be at the apex of all these trends because their legislation and constitutions could — and did — apply the models of the most advanced countries. These laws were frequently destined to become dead letters, as reality caught up with hope and illusion. But part of the achievement of a sense of a reality was the need to gain the experience of what was economically and socially possible, and what was not. All this could be only dimly perceived in the 1940s, or even in the 1950s.

Early in the postwar period it was clear that all too many of the new nations did not have — or would not have for at least decades — economic viability. Economic forces operating over centuries played a well-known role in shaping the industrialized nations. Nations like India, China, and Egypt had existed long before the modern industrial leaders. In any cultural or historical sense, they were very old, not "new" nations. But many had undergone major transformations in the decades or centuries preceding their reassertion of independence in the twentieth century. The orientation of the colonies had been toward "mother" countries, and their economic viability was an integral element of a larger entity — the British, the French, the Dutch, and other empires. Moreover, generally speaking, they lagged behind in industrialization, infrastructure, and modernization of domestic food production. The desire to be a separate, independent nation dominated state-making, not economic viability. Nations were to be made of areas that had been created only by the great-power rivalries and compromises that led to arbitrary divisions of territories within Asia and Africa. The careful planning for British Commonwealth status, which had been so evident as late as the mid-1930s, was to give way to an unrestrained expression of the principle of self-determination. World War II had accentuated nationalistic feelings; the imitation effect was very strong and few colonial powers wished to be in the position of thwarting nationalistic aspirations.

The new states, it was obvious, would require external financial and technical assistance from the industrial countries, particularly the United States and the former "mother" countries. Thus, countries came into existence with the prior knowledge of all concerned that, for the indefinite future, many — if not all — would require external assistance. These countries were eager to accelerate economic and social development, but they lacked the economic basis for achieving these objectives without large-scale continuous assistance from higher-income countries.

Some, particularly India and Egypt, did have accumulated foreign-exchange balances as a result of wartime expenditures in their countries by the Allies. Pound sterling and U.S. dollar balances could not be spent during the war because of supply scarcities; as a result these accumulations were very large, equivalent in purchasing power to tens of billions of 1971–72 U.S. dollars. Similar accumulations were held by others of the low-income countries, especially those in Latin America. These sterling and dollar balances were, in effect, debts of the United Kingdom and the United States. Use of sterling balances was expected to present a likely source of major difficulties for the United Kingdom after the war. A significant portion of Britain's exports would be paid for with accumulated sterling balances. Britain would have to pay cash in foreign currency for much of its own imports, while much of its exports would be paid for by sterling holders using these balances; this reduced Britain's debts but did not produce the cash needed to pay for imports. The sterling balances proved, however, small compared with the demands for imports in the countries holding them; they would be largely used up by the mid-1950s.

The use of dollar balances by Latin American countries paralleled the story of sterling balances. No one, however, worried about the ability of the United States to provide the resources in exchange for these dollars, or that the U.S. would not earn enough foreign exchange to pay for its imports. These were to be the years of world "dollar shortage." The weight of concern was as to whether there would be too few, not too many, U.S. dollars in the hands of countries outside the United States. The world "dollar glut" of the 1960s and 1970s was not even dimly seen.

Although the need for external assistance to the low-income countries had been recognized in the 1940s, it was to be many years before the duration and magnitude of that need would be recognized. That these new nations would be a net drain on the world's available productive resources was obvious. It should have strengthened expectations of high levels of world demand relative to world supply.

6

The International
Economic System

The Bretton Woods Psychology

The post–World War II period started with one major distinct advantage. The war, as it had taught many other things, had also taught the benefits of effective international cooperation, economically and financially, as well as militarily. Lend-lease, extended by the United States for example, was designed to enable the Allies to obtain assistance from the United States without incurring huge amounts of debt. It truly reflected the concept of "alliance," with each member contributing what it could to the common cause of victory. Lend-lease avoided the burdens and bitterness that grew out of the war loans of World War I. Looking into the future, it was obvious that international economic, financial, and monetary cooperation could ease the giant task of postwar reconstruction and of re-creation of a viable world economy — something which, by 1945, had not existed for over fifteen years, and even in the 1920s had shown great weaknesses.

The Allied governments came together, at Bretton Woods in 1944, to design international institutions that would be at the center of postwar international economic relations: the International Monetary Fund and the World Bank. The International Monetary Fund was to restore a system of relationships among national currencies that would help achieve the postwar objectives of expanding employment, output, and international trade; the World Bank was to help re-establish the international investment and flows of capital deemed necessary to achieve these same objectives. From the perspective of the deep concern with depression, it is perhaps not surprising that the problems posed by the prospect of persistent inflation were neglected. The system designed at Bretton Woods was, however, to prove vulnerable to those very problems — particularly when they developed in the major trading countries.

Given the profound impact on national and world prosperity of international trade and exchange of goods, arrangements for the payments for such trade take on critical importance. Such payments arrangements are usually referred to as international monetary relations and include the prices at which national currencies exchange for one another, that is, exchange rates, and the markets in which such exchanges take place, foreign exchange markets. Particularly in view of the experience with the collapse of world trade in the 1930s, it is not surprising that the need was felt during World War II for agreement on rules and mechanisms to govern international monetary relations. Other international economic relations were also very important, of which international trade itself merits explicit mentioning, and efforts were made in this area also. But the international monetary system is uniquely important because it is the mechanism involved in all other relations, and the rules in this area apply directly to the pursuit of the domestic objective of full employment.

The International Monetary Fund serves as the center of the postwar international monetary system. Its Articles of Agreement climaxed a series of both informal and formal meetings which began in 1942. Various countries, including the United Kingdom, the United States, the Soviet Union, developing countries like India, Egypt, and China, those in Latin America, and the European governments-in-exile like France, Czechoslovakia, Belgium, Netherlands, and Norway, took part. A new international monetary system was needed and the United States took the lead in proposing one. The United Kingdom also made major proposals and its views greatly influenced the final agreement, with a number of countries having some impact, for example, Canada and France. Though the United States took the lead in proposing the new system, the U.S. position was a reflection of what came to be called Keynesian economics. Lord Keynes himself was the senior member of the British team which deliberated on these new proposals.

This is not the place to write a history or detailed critique of the international monetary system or even of the International Monetary Fund. Both have been the subjects of separate volumes; but they deserve some discussion here as the deliberations leading to the formation of the Fund reflected some of the concerns already outlined. Most important, perhaps, was the fear of a possible relapse into a great depression, once the immediate postwar adjustment period had come to an end.

The Experience of the 1930s

The international monetary system had failed utterly in the 1930s to provide the framework for the revival of national economies, international trade, and international investment ravaged by depression. The collapse of the international monetary system prolonged, spread, and deepened the Great Depression. Instead of effective international cooperation, countries sought to shelter themselves from the prolonged world-wide economic storm without regard to the harmful effects of their actions on other countries.

In some countries, imports were kept out by controls, high tariffs, or other government restrictions; even by the deplorable employment standards of the 1930s, it was not possible to reduce imports to match declines in exports without increasing unemployment even more and contracting domestic demand. Exporters lost desperately needed markets, even while their own domestic markets continued to shrink as the 1930s moved on. Parallel "beggar-thy-neighbor" policies took place in the field of international investment. Balance-of-payments difficulties, greatly increased by demand for foreign exchange coming from people eager to protect themselves against spreading political disorder and war by building up nest eggs abroad, resulted in widespread defaults on foreign indebtedness, private and governmental. Foreign investment dwindled. At the very time when more business enterprise was needed to increase investment and income, the international climate drastically discouraged risk taking.

Moreover, under these conditions, countries tried to prosper unfairly at the expense of others by following practices which gave them an artificial competitive advantage over other countries in exporting. A principal device for doing this was simply to devalue their national money in terms of other currencies. The importer had to pay more of the national currency to buy foreign exchange to pay for imports. In terms of his own currency — which matters most because the imported goods will be sold in his own country for domestic currency — imports became more expensive. Therefore, he bought fewer imports. On the opposite side, the exporter from the devaluing country was able to sell the foreign exchange he earned from his sales abroad for more of his own currency — even if, in foreign currency, the foreign price remained the same. In domestic currency, the exporter's profits increased. Therefore, if he had to beat some competitor, he could now afford to lower his foreign price in foreign currencies, hopefully from his viewpoint, to make sales he might otherwise forfeit to some foreign competitor. The exporting country was helped at the expense of others.

In the world of the 1930s, countries felt forced to defend themselves against such exports cheapened by devaluation of the exporting country's currency. They did so by any of several means. Some devalued their own currencies in retaliation; some restricted imports by imposing direct controls or prohibitively high tariffs. Others achieved offsetting devaluation by permitting their exchange rates to "float," the rate being determined only by the demand and supply for foreign exchange coming into the market. Massive unemployment and economic stagnation spread from country to country.

All such exchange-rate practices contrasted sharply with the nearly universal practice of the late nineteenth and early twentieth centuries: to maintain a fixed value for a national currency in terms of gold. In this way, the exchange rate would be "neutral," that is, not providing competitive advantage to any country over another, but merely linking national economies and their currencies efficiently. Changes in a country's economic conditions which affected its balance of payments and international competitiveness were not to result in changes in its exchange rate but rather in its re-adjustment in domestic economic conditions. That was the dominant characteristic of the gold standard or its post–World War I revised version, the gold-exchange standard.

Gold movements were the ultimate means of settling balance-of-payments deficits, i.e., the differences between the total receipts from foreign nations and total payments to foreign nations. The change in gold supply laid the basis for further automatic changes in money and income, and ultimately in prices. Exchange rates were fixed and stable. The alternative, devaluation of the foreign-exchange value of a currency to offset rising costs and prices and so to increase domestic currency earnings from exports, was not available under the prevailing "rules of the game." In essence, under that standard, adjustments in the deficit country — falling income, money supply, and prices — were paralleled by opposite adjustments in the surplus country. Balance and competitiveness tended *automatically* to return to the system.

In practice, countries did come to use currencies, predominantly the British pound sterling, as well as gold, to meet deficits. In time, countries also devised means of insulating their domestic economies, at least partially, from the balance of payments. This they did by holding a stock of foreign-exchange assets, internationally acceptable for settling balance-of-payments deficits, separated from the domestic money supply. And, with a stock of international reserves, balance-of-payments deficits could endure much longer than when adjustment was (supposedly) automatic. But these assets — gold and foreign currencies that are today called "international monetary reserves" when held by the central bank — were limited in amount and not easily augmented by borrowing when the borrowing countries were experiencing economic and financial difficulties. In any case the avoidance of prolonged or large balance-of-payments deficits was regarded as essential, even if this required either strong measures to avoid increasing domestic demand and rising costs and prices, or drastic measures, including substantially increased unemployment, to reduce domestic demand and reduce costs and prices.

The system, particularly the gold standard in its pre–World War I form, had (as it is remembered at least) operated as a powerful pressure against the continuation of price inflation. It encouraged international competitiveness by providing incentives to improve productivity and efficiency. It penalized cost and price rises, and precluded manipulation of exchange rates as a means of maintaining a competitive position, despite cost and price increases larger than in competitor countries. It provided the certainty about exchange rates that was regarded as an essential prerequisite for the expansion of world trade which, in turn, was regarded as essential for domestic expansion and prosperity.

Great Britain attempted in the 1920s to return to a modified gold standard, but at the pre–World War I exchange rate despite the important economic and financial changes brought about by World War I and its immediate aftermath. This was regarded as a principal cause of economic stagnation and continued large-scale unemployment in Great Britain during the 1920s. This experience with prolonged unemployment gave many Englishmen the same kind of fear of an automatic international monetary system based on a fixed exchange rate and limited access to international reserves that the runaway inflation after World War I had given many Germans. Germans view the recurrence of such inflation as the worst economic calamity. Englishmen are horrified by the thought of unemployment. These experiences are part of the cultural heritage of modern Britain and Germany and still largely influence thinking and policies there and elsewhere.

The United Kingdom in 1931, the United States in 1933, and Japan in 1934 gave up the fixed relation of their currencies to gold in the hope of getting more freedom of action to pursue expansionary economic policies. Their currencies were allowed to "float" or "fluctuate": the foreign price for sterling, the most important internationally used currency at that time, was determined essentially by the international supply of and demand for sterling. International supply and demand met in various financial centers — not only in London, but also in New York, Paris, and Zurich — where the international financial transactions requiring the buying or selling of sterling took place. Neither deficits nor surpluses can persist under this mechanism because the supply and demend for the currency are made equal by changes in the exchange rates.

The experiment in floating rates proved unsuccessful.

Countries used this freedom of action to try to maintain competitive advantages in shrinking world markets and to make it more difficult for others to sell in their own home markets. For a short period it seemed to work, even if at the expense of other countries, but not for long. Freedom of action given to all merely meant that any change by one country could be offset by a counterbalancing change in another.

After the years of experimentation in the 1930s, the major currencies were found much in the same relation to each other as before. But uncertainty as to the future values of currencies seriously handicapped the revival of international trade and the flows of financial capital needed to help restore the world economy. After a few years countries took steps to try to achieve stability in their exchange markets and made international arrangements to assist each other in such efforts. The Tripartite Agreement among the United States, Britain, and France in 1936 was the outstanding example of this. The United States, Britain, and France undertook to abstain from deliberate, excessive depreciation of their exchange rates and to consult with each other if they were to find it impossible to continue to refrain from such actions. The Tripartite Agreement thus inspired the proposals formulated in the early 1940s which were to culminate in the Bretton Woods Agreement.

The International Monetary Fund

The experiences of the 1930s were very vivid in the memories of those who participated in the international discussion

and negotiations beginning in 1942 and climaxing in the
Bretton Woods Conference in 1944. All felt the need for a
fund of international credits to allow countries to meet temporary balance-of-payments deficits without resorting to
measures "destructive of international prosperity." The
United Kingdom and others would have preferred a fund of
virtually unlimited size; the United States, however, favored
a fund of much more limited though still quite large proportions. These funds were intended to enable governments
that were now accepting the responsibility to avoid serious
prolonged unemployment to work for what came to be
called "full employment." Simultaneously, there was to be
an international bank to help revive the flow of international
investment. Taken together these institutions would bring
economic growth instead of the economic stagnation which
had characterized the Great Depression.

In retrospect, the war also provided important and propitious elements for reaching a successful and comprehensive
agreement on a postwar international monetary system. The
global character of the war meant that peacetime international financial relations had virtually ceased. What trade
took place was largely under lend-lease; foreign-exchange
markets were closed and intergovernmental financial settle-
ments were arranged bilaterally between central banks.
International movement of privately held funds was made
very difficult; nearly all foreign-exchange markets were
closed. Thus the wartime situation itself eliminated fears
of adverse effects on foreign-exchange markets and on exchange rates from discussions on monetary reform.

In the international monetary field it was finally agreed

that countries would, under specified conditions, have access to a pool of funds which could be used to meet temporary balance-of-payments deficits. The pool was to consist of a collection contributed by the member countries of their national currencies and some gold amounting to an internationally agreed total — $8.8 billion originally. The United States was the largest contributor — $2.75 billion; the United Kindom contributed $1.3 billion. Provision was made to increase this total if deemed desirable in the future.

The pool of funds was to be managed by the International Monetary Fund. Forty-five countries were original signatories to the Fund's Articles of Agreement and all but the Soviet Union eventually joined.

A member country experiencing a temporary balance-of-payments deficit might sell the Fund its own national currency, up to specified limits, in exchange for the foreign currencies it needed. Each country could presumably obtain its own national currency either from its budget or from its central bank. The basic assumption is that any currency sold in exchange for another will at some future date be purchased by still another country, or "repurchased" by the country that had initially sold it. Repurchase simply means that the country buys back its national currency which it previously sold to the pool to obtain a needed foreign currency. To buy back its own currency, it uses foreign currencies acceptable to the Fund; thereby it replenishes the pool. The IMF is, therefore, a "revolving" fund; its composition changes as currencies are bought and sold, but the total monetary value of its resources remains the same.

Today's world has grown accustomed to rapidly expanding international trade. It is hard to imagine the nightmares caused by the economic policies of the 1930s. One lesson seemed clear: competitive exchange-rate depreciation was a mechanism for spreading economic unemployment and economic disaster. This fear led to the adoption of the principles in the Bretton Woods Agreement that exchange rates were again to be fixed and that changes in them would be a matter for international consultation and decision. Exchange-rate changes were, moreover, to be made, not because of temporary changes in business conditions, but because basic and lasting change had come about in the country's economy that was causing a "fundamental disequilibrium" in its balance of payments.

The Fund Agreement attempted to combine some of the more attractive features of the gold standard — exchange-rate stability and freedom from exchange restrictions — with more flexibility in changing exchange rates and access to international funds. At the same time, the frustrations of the 1930s experience with floating exchange rates and depression-encouraging measures were to be avoided.

The World Bank

The other major institution designed during the war to help achieve postwar prosperity and agreed to at Bretton Woods was the International Bank for Reconstruction and Development. As set forth in its Articles of Agreement, the Bank was to assist in the reconstruction and development of territories of members by facilitating the investment of capital for productive purposes; these included the restoration of economies destroyed or disrupted by the war, the reconversion of productive facilities to peacetime needs, and the encouragement of the development of the productive facilities and resources in the less developed countries. Preoccupation with the same kinds of concerns as were reflected in the Fund Agreement was clearly evident in the Bank's statement of purpose: "To promote the long-range balanced growth of international trade and the maintenance of equilibrium in balance of payments by encouraging international investment for the development of the productive resources of members, thereby assisting in raising productivity, the standard of living and conditions of labor in their territories." Among other things, the Bank would supplement private investment. When private capital was not available on reasonable terms, the Bank would provide finance out of its own capital, either by raising funds or from its other resources, such as earnings on loans.

The original capital of the Bank, contributed by member countries, was intended to amount to $9.1 billion. As in the case of the Fund, the Soviet Union was an original signatory at Bretton Woods, but did not join. The United States subscribed nearly 40 percent of the capital — $3175 million; the United Kingdom was the only other country subscribing over $1 billion in capital — $1300 million. From the beginning of its operations in 1946, it was clear that the need for capital was much greater than the Bank's resources. The Bank saw itself as a "catalyst" to stimulate production and encourage private investment, and as a general "helpful" influence in, for example, achieving the removal of unnecessary trade barriers. But the Bank did not have sufficient funds to finance the reconstruction of war-devastated countries. This helps explain the need for the Marshall Plan.

The International Trade Organization

During World War II, it had been assumed that nations would adopt an international trade agreement, parallel to the Fund and Bank agreements, which would devise a set of rules to encourage expansion of trade and to make the imposition of trade barriers, tariff and nontariff alike, a matter of international concern and action. This view was explicitly endorsed at Bretton Woods. Tariffs and other forms of trade restriction had, in the United States and elsewhere, played a major role in the sharp decline of world trade in the 1930s.

An international trade agreement was, in fact, considered at a number of conferences, and a charter for the International Trade Organization was drawn up at a conference in Havana in 1946. The charter was discussed at subsequent meetings. But by 1948 it was too late. What had been done in the international monetary and investment fields — in an atmosphere of despair mixed with euphoria, of determination not to repeat past failures of the twenties and thirties and yet of hope for the future, and in recognition of the incalculable, astronomically large war destruction of productive facilities — could no longer be done in the field of international trade. The time was no longer propitious for a full-blown international agreement.

Instead, the lesser, but still useful, General Agreement on Tariffs and Trade (GATT) came into being. It provided general rules regarding the use of tariff and nontariff barriers, and a mechanism for discussion and negotiation among member countries. And, over time, the GATT has become more useful than its original supporters had ever dared to hope. Major international agreements to reduce tariffs were arranged under its auspices, the last being the so-called Kennedy Round. The GATT also helped to reduce the use of import quotas and gain recognition for the special problems of the poorer nations.

7

1945 in Retrospect

The Attitude Toward Inflation

Except for some isolated examples after World War I, like the German inflation, widespread and persistent inflation had not been experienced for centuries. Even those who feared postwar inflation usually saw it as peculiar to the most devastated areas and inherently temporary, lasting only until wartime devastation had been repaired. Those concerned primarily with inflation tended to side with those who argued for some return to the "discipline" of the gold standard. This view was taken by a few academic and financial experts, but most saw this fear as simply anachronistic by 1945.

Indeed, so widespread was the assumption that persistent inflation would not be a problem that the international monetary system that was adopted was — and clearly remains — vulnerable to destruction if persistent inflation emerged in many countries, particularly the more important countries economically. Key principles of the Fund are threatened by persistent widespread inflation — the system of "fixed parities" most of all, but also the constraints placed on use of governmental controls (exchange restrictions) to reduce foreign payments for goods and services. With persistent inflation countries cannot abide by the Fund rules on exchange rates and avoidance of exchange restrictions; the limited size of the pool threatens repeatedly to become inadequate to meet the simultaneous needs of a number of countries in balance-of-payments difficulties.

Where countries would repeatedly need international support to finance temporary balance-of-payments deficits, the managers of the system could and did insist on "stabilization programs" to reduce or eliminate inflationary pressures. But, for countries which did not require such assistance repeatedly — and this was true of most of the industrial countries — the system had to rely on its other brakes: fixed exchange rates and avoidance of exchange restrictions. As will be seen later, the continuation for decades of a U.S. balance-of-payments deficit meant that other industrial countries usually were in balance-of-payments surplus and had no need for international assistance. Moreover, the U.S. itself made little use of the Fund's facilities.

The Disastrous Blunder of 1945

The world was not prepared to deal with postwar problems because only the more obvious and direct consequences of the war were generally recognized; the profound but less obvious forces for change were ignored or neglected. Destruction of productive capacity in a number of industrialized countries was only partly offset by the increased capacity in the United States and Canada. There was, too, an unknown but huge backlog of demand for consumer and investment goods; demand had been pent up for many years of war and depression. Often savings were available, ready to make the demand for consumer and capital goods effective, and banking systems were eager to get back to the business of peacetime lending. Some did expect a temporary boom immediately after the war. But, what was not seen and even now is only vaguely understood is that the other factors which came out of the war, or reached fruition during it, would release expansionary forces in the postwar period that had no historical precedents. Full employment would become a sine qua non of national policy and the scope of social legislation would be widely extended; government would play an ever larger role, with attendant increases in expenditure and taxation levels. Rising expectations, new definitions of material well-being would supplant older concepts of tolerable poverty. New, more advanced means of communication would facilitate widespread, nearly instantaneous imitation by countries and peoples of each other, multiplying by many times the "demonstration" effect of changes in consumer tastes or technology. The Americanization of consumption and production would really be worldwide in content as well as in application. Industrial and market structures would change, and trade unions would gather new importance, acceptance, and power. With all this, the end of war failed to bring an era of comfortable peace. Instead, it ushered in a costly Cold War. Amidst this, many new nations were to become sovereign states.

The inflation growing out of all these events could not be short-lived. Business cycles would be very different; they would take place in an inflationary environment. The general levels of national prices might be affected by business cycles but their trend would be usually upward.

Unfortunately, only a few saw this, and even fewer perceived its serious implications. The strength of expansionary forces was underestimated and inflation was seen as temporary, and manageable by the accepted techniques to deal with temporary inflation — a disastrous blunder in analysis and judgment. Even the dramatic collapse of the Nationalist government of China on the mainland in the 1940s, due largely to the all-pervasive, corrosive, destructive social and political effects of many years of continuous inflation, was not read as a lesson for others. China was "unique" in many respects, but not in the causes and the all-important effects of persistent inflation.

Hiroshima initiated a period of apocalyptic visions, visions of world destruction by nuclear bomb, and measures were taken to avoid this all-consuming horror. At the same time, quite from the opposite direction, was a vision of the economically possible, a vision that made Victorian optimism shameful for its caution and tolerance of slowness and gradualness. But the new prosperity could also poison the world — if not with bombs, with pollution of air and water. It could destroy cities, the traditional centers of progress. And inflation could steadily erode the very gains the new economic efforts and policies were designed to achieve. The postwar period had begun with a well-conceived strategy to overcome the prewar economic problems, but there was no second line of defense to deal with the consequences of its success. Little wonder! The powerful expansionary forces released to burgeon into that success were for most people, blinded by their prewar perspective, beyond comprehension.

The postwar world has sought various objectives. But it is

not yet aware of the devastating obstacles to achieving these objectives inherent in continuing or persistent inflation. There is a confusion between temporary and continuing inflation. A new and major error is therefore in the making, as serious as that made in the 1940s and 1950s in underestimating the strength of world demand for governmental purposes, private consumption, and investment.

The new error lies in the definition of the problem: the problem is seen as a choice between "inflation" and the new objectives of the postwar world. Believing itself faced with this choice, the world, perhaps understandably, has largely chosen to ignore inflation or to regard it as an inevitable cost, however undesirable, of the pursuit of great national objectives. What is wrong is the conclusion that a choice must be made.

There is no choice. To choose inflation is to accept *in advance* failure to achieve these great national objectives and, instead, to create the very conditions that undermine the progress toward those objectives. It is like choosing nuclear war to "save" civilization. The problem is how to manage economies so that national objectives are made consistent with the elimination of persistent inflation.

III

The 1950s and 1960s:
an Overview

8

The Creation of
Chronic Excess Demand

Political and Social Realities

With European and Japanese reconstruction nearly completed by the early 1950s — at least as measured by the restoration of prewar productive capacities — increasing attention in Europe and somewhat less in Japan focused on the problems of price and wage rises. But inflation proved more intractable and obdurate than might have been expected even from the many signs present in the late 1940s. It is easy to assume that stubborn, widespread inflation is symptomatic of new conditions and problems requiring that it be stoically accepted. For myself, this is unproved and unwarranted pessimism.

To deal effectively with persistent inflation, we have to begin by agreeing on what the key economic, social, and political realities of the postwar world are and try to grapple with them. Postwar price and cost trends, the persistency of modern inflation in so many countries, cannot be understood unless the major social and political aspects of modern societies are viewed simultaneously with the economic. Narrower explanations, like changes in money supply, may seem

to explain changes in prices, but there are too many changes
that remain unexplained. Modern societies have transformed
definitions of acceptable poverty, of tolerable unemployment, of equitable income distribution, of decent living
standards, of spiritual fulfillment, and of governmental responsibilities for the achievement and maintenance of all
these. This transformation went on in the 1950s and 1960s.
It is still going on.

Furthermore, the Cold War, coming on the heels of
World War II, was itself a major expansionary force. But it
is not possible to separate one expansionary force and label it
"the" cause of excessive demand and inflation. The Cold
War coexisted with the burgeoning of new nations, the
transformed social outlook throughout the world, and the
increased, and still increasing, private consumption that accompanies higher aspirations and rising incomes. And the
new definition of governmental responsibilities and areas of
activities — with the resultant massive increases in the size of
governmental expenditures, taxation, and public borrowing
(where governments have the credit standing to borrow) —
have become major factors in the economic behavior of individuals, firms, industries, and national economies. Clearly, it
is the combination that creates the excess. Modern government has still not learned how to extend successfully the
responsibilities of government to encompass the social and
economic management of society. Yet governments are expected to fulfill massive responsibilities to numbers of people
undreamed of, even in the last century, and increasing rapidly. Governments took hundreds of years to learn how to
do effectively the relatively few things that were regarded as

their responsibilities and for much smaller numbers of people. Modern technologies assist government, by improving communication and facilitating travel. Fundamentally, however, what we have are governments grappling with major new responsibilities in areas where human experience is limited and where what experience we have may be inapplicable in a world of nearly 4 billion people made economically one by modern communication and transportation. From this, we can begin to understand why we live in an age of scarcity despite huge increased capacity.

Expectations of society outrun its ability to produce. Moreover, government is confidently expected to ensure that these expectations are realized. It requires little imagination to create sufficient demand to attain full employment. Much imagination — more than people and countries have shown thus far — is required to manage that demand so that persistent inflation and unemployment do not result simultaneously. Unemployment can easily result by misdirection of demand and supply, through errors of judgment on how to manage demand so as to avoid undesired, persistent increases in prices and costs.

Soaring Consumption

In retrospect, perhaps the most important phenomenon of the postwar period has been the magnitude of demand for consumer goods. Not only the depression and war, but most of the events of the past one hundred to two hundred years set the stage for the surging consumer demand that has typified the postwar years.

After World War II, the demand for consumption dramatically altered in a number of dimensions. Some products — automobiles, houses, refrigerators, cosmetics, clothing, radios — became ever more elaborate and subject to frequent changes in styling and technology. Simultaneously, new products — television, dishwashers, clothes dryers, countless small appliances and gadgets — entered into common consumption patterns. The market for these products seemed ever expanding. There were more people; many had higher incomes. And consumption per family increased. Because products were used more intensively, or deteriorated faster, they required more frequent repair, if not replacement.

One dramatic illustration of the change in consumption habits is travel. The airplane has not only made travel physically possible, but travel is now within reach, not only of the once well-publicized, wealthy "jet set," but of the rapidly expanding higher-income classes of Europe, Japan, and North America — to say nothing of their offspring. In a few years, what was the prerogative of the wealthy has become an ordinary event. With more travelers visiting more places, still other demands arise: for hotels and restaurants, expanded airports and roads, for drinkable water and sanitary facilities in areas where these are luxuries for the ordinary residents, for cultural and sports festivals to attract tourists, for travel literature, for "appropriate" clothing and sports equipment, for special schools to teach managers, counselors, and guides. Tourism has become a major world-wide industry, jumping over national frontiers and scornful of barriers such as thousands of miles of ocean or jungle. And this is but one example.

What had started before World War II as the Americanization of world consumption by a slow process of imitation accelerated into a frenzy of everybody imitating everybody else. Anything "foreign" is more chic everywhere than anything "domestic." Advertising, in all media, fosters this frenzy. Consumers are lured into decisions they are told will satiate some basic psychological or physiological need — one perhaps only remotely related to the particular product. The popularization of Freudian psychology opened new vistas to merchandising products; conscious or subconscious sexual needs can be implicitly or explicitly satisfied with products previously regarded as merely satisfying some simple obvious or conscious need. Automobiles are sold as sex symbols, and airline stewardesses parade like the burlesque queens of previous eras.

The postwar change in consumer attitudes is the result of more than mass advertising, mass production, and mass selling; it also reflects mass consumer-credit facilities. These are relatively easily, if expensively, obtained. They are advertised and sold like consumer products. Individual tastes and consumption demand need no longer be (and indeed are not) directly related to income, or even to expectations of income. The result is ever-increasing demand for consumer commodities and services.

Governments, even when dismayed by the presence of inflation, make use of this attitude toward consumption, when confronted by politically and socially defined intolerable unemployment or lower rates of growth; repeatedly, they stimulate the economy by encouraging still more consumption. Where a relative decline in capital expenditures — in investment — used to be an urgent warning of imminent

economic recession or economic stagnation, failure to stimulate consumption now sends tremors through the economic
world. For we have come to rely on seemingly insatiable
consumption to revive declining economies and to do so with
little delay — before unemployment becomes prolonged or
severe. Out of this emphasis comes the demand for steadily
rising money incomes, for without the prospect of increased
money incomes the bubbles burst. Rising prices increase the
demand for rising incomes. Thus, the need for ever-increasing money income becomes greater, many people may well
find themselves consuming less and less, despite increased
money income or greater debts. Consumption has taken on
an orgiastic character. The results are by no means all bad,
particularly for those able to satisfy their demands despite
rising prices. But many, lacking income or credit, remain
frustrated and increasingly discontented. In this process of
artificially induced demand and excessive debt, the producer
and the consumer whose income cannot keep up with the
persistent inflation pay the piper.

*New Conceptions: Employment, Unemployment,
and Welfare and Consumer Demand*

The postwar world has formulated new definitions of "serious" or "prolonged" unemployment. Gone are the days
when a depression was expected to bring unemployment up
to 10 to 20 percent in an industrial country. Outside of the
United States, governments find levels of 2 or 3 percent
unemployment regarded by their people as unacceptable;
before the war, such figures would have been evidence of

prosperity. Even in the United States, with its large pockets of hard-core unemployment, prosperity means something between 3 to 4 percent unemployment, recession something between 5 to 7 percent.

Once a definition of acceptable or unacceptable employment becomes prevalent, governments seriously (or rather, certainly) jeopardize their continuance in office, if — except for very brief periods — they allow unemployment levels to exceed accepted limits. These limits greatly restrict the freedom of action to cope with changing conditions. A strong commitment to an overall or average unemployment target, commendable in many respects, does limit the availability of labor for opening industries in new areas or the desire to decrease armament expenditures to release resources for other purposes. This does not argue against full employment. Indeed, for me a major objection to permitting the continuation of persistent inflation is that eventually it makes impossible the achievement of employment objectives. It does argue for understanding the implications of any given full-employment approach.

Similarly, the concepts of welfare and the scope of social legislation have gone well beyond immediate postwar expectations. Governments feel a responsibility for the material well-being of their people. In many countries, governments make some money payments, or their equivalent, to those who cannot earn their livelihood. Many remember when governments did not feel this responsibility. Individuals may have felt concerned and responsible, and governments may have deplored the existence of deprivation. Some may even have tried by general measures to improve economic conditions. But the lot of the individual was not government's responsibility. There were few exceptions, for example, the provision of education (varying among the countries), water supply, and some minimal responsibilities for eradication of widespread diseases like malaria and the plague. Indeed, only fairly recently has it even become commonly accepted that the supplying of certain services like urban transport and electricity are governmental responsibilities.

Most nations have been deeply affected by the new concepts of governmental responsibility for the welfare of people. The impoverished reached by the new welfare systems number in the tens of millions in the United States alone, and are increasing markedly and steadily everywhere.

The improvement in the condition of the impoverished has become a modern social and political imperative. Depriving large numbers of people of government relief or allowing mass deprivation to persist — even if it were theoretically possible — is simply neither socially nor politically acceptable or feasible. Whatever its faults, this is an age of deepening concern for people. But, like abolishing large-scale unemployment, that concern has social costs which must be recognized, as well as benefits. It does not usually add to the short-term productive capacity of a nation, though it may add much in the longer run. In the short run (measured in years, not months), it further widens the gap between demand and available supply.

In addition, a new attitude prevails, one which fundamentally changes our concepts of "effective demand." Hitherto demand was "effective" only if people could pay, currently or eventually, for what they wanted. The ability to pay came from income, earned by participating in the productive process as factory workers, farmers, salesmen, managers, investors. Demand which could not be made "effective" by earned income could be largely ignored. No longer is this so: income need not be earned. This changes one of the fundamental assumptions of economic thinking. Private firms understand this, but the public and their governments have not faced up to its consequences for the nation as a whole.

Education for All

Nor is demand restricted to consumer goods. The education "explosion" in the postwar period has also been quite spectacular. The GI Bill of Rights in the United States acted as a catalytic force in a revolution of educational expectations. First, general financial support for education was available only to veterans. But the idea of publicly assisted higher education in the United States took root and became a standard. Other nations have done likewise. The figures for attendance at universities in all countries are staggering relative to prewar standards, whether in industrial countries like France, Italy, or Sweden, or in developing countries like Brazil, India, Chile, Nigeria, and Turkey. These numbers are usually counted in the tens of thousands per university, instead of the previous hundreds or few thousands. Not only are universities much bigger than ever, but their expansion has been far more rapid than expected, making it difficult to maintain traditional educational standards with buildings, libraries, and student accommodation drastically inadequate or inferior to previous periods.

Government-supported public education is on such an enlarged scale as to make both the product, and its implications for the economy, quite new. It is one of the world's largest industries. Education has become a "right" and in many countries this "right" extends through university and professional schools. Government budgets have been stretched and further stretched to meet the modern demands for education at all levels from "preschool" to graduate school. The nineteenth-century proponents of "free education" could hardly have foreseen the unbelievable success of their efforts. Everywhere more people attend school and there are demands not only that education be accessible to ever-broadening sections of the population, but that the scope and quality of research and instruction be improved as well.

Virtually nowhere, however, are nations able to implement this approach by providing the resources which will enable the education systems to do their jobs well. In practice, the demands for education are not met, either as formulated or in the minds of the public. Limitations, enforced particularly by the desire to avoid higher taxes, or by unwillingness to shift consumption priorities, result in acceptance of less than the best. Nonetheless, the pressures to meet new standards are there all the time, and mounting steadily. The public everywhere is repeatedly disappointed, despite the ever-increasing educational budgets.

This feeling of disappointment extends beyond aspects covered in government budgets like number of teachers and buildings. New activities of government, as well as of private institutions, cause individuals to look to others to determine their talents, to sort out their objectives in life, to relate the two, and to obtain, formally or informally, the needed skills and education. Government agencies not only help determine people's potentials, identify their skills, suggest careers and learning institutions; they are also expected to provide significant proportions of the financing needed for the growing numbers of students. Further, government, by being the largest single employer, greatly, if indirectly, can influence the career decisions of individuals. Many people become teachers, scientists, computer technicians because governments encourage people to enter these fields. This is a far cry from choosing a career by following in Dad's footsteps or by responding to an inner-felt call to pursue a certain profession. Compounding the problem, after encouraging people to pursue certain professional programs, governments often find that they have miscalculated; the available talent is not needed. These are not errors of stupidity or malice, but are due to the virtual impossibility of accurate prediction and of quick adaptation of individual choices of career to unexpected changes in opportunities. Needless to say, the government is held responsible for the consequent frustrations and personal difficulties.

Thus, the governments find themselves on the horns of a dilemma — to meet the demands for more and better education and thereby to incur the public's wrath for the seeming inadequacies and errors of judgment as well as high costs, or, alternatively, to refuse to meet these demands and reduce their responsibilities and thereby be regarded as totally unresponsive to their people's needs. Governments have chosen a muddle of the two.

Defense Expenditures at Wartime Levels

Had no other responsibilities been assumed by modern governments, armament expenditures alone would have had significant expansionary, if not inflationary impacts on their economies.

Moreover, the Cold War, predictable in its general effects, has persisted. The armaments' burden, which increased military expenditures, came on top of already rising levels of governmental expenditures and rising demand for private consumption and investment. Consequently, they heightened inflation to a much greater extent than can be seen by merely comparing the relative sizes of military expenditures in these wars with those in World War II. Armament expenditures are not only largely nonproductive, but they have been huge — amounting to about 200 billion dollars per year for all countries taken together. This nearly equals the combined output of France and the United Kingdom. In the United States alone, such expenditures have been of the order of 5 to 10 percent of the total gross national product, not too different from total expenditure on new construction or on consumption of durable goods. Moreover, defense expenditures not only inherently strengthen the trend toward reduced competition in markets; they further exacerbate the existing difficulties of national economic management.

During both the Korean and Vietnam wars many argued

that the U.S. government ought to deal with the consequent inflationary pressure as it had in World War II: by comprehensive, detailed, and direct price, wage, production, and consumption controls. The alternative to controls was to reduce consumption and investment in nonmilitary goods by taxation and other fiscal measures. But particularly in the case of the Vietnam war, the U.S. government did not call on its people to sacrifice on behalf of military victory. The inflationary consequences were widely underestimated or ignored.

Following World War II, other wars had had serious inflationary consequences. The French wars in Indo-China and Algeria were a major factor in the chronic weaknesses of the French economy in the 1950s. It was not until these wars had been ended that the French economy obtained the strength which it increasingly demonstrated in the 1960s. The United Kingdom was also confronted by the burden of a large military budget in the 1950s. Here, again, the military figures by themselves would not appear large. But, in an economy already unable to harmonize national objectives of very low levels of unemployment, satisfactory growth rates, and acceptable balance-of-payments performance, the military expenditures were nonetheless important. The United Kingdom, therefore, reduced its armament expenditures and military commitments, particularly in the Middle East and Asia.

Germany and Japan, kept virtually free of significant military expenditure, became vivid examples of the strength of expansionary forces in the second half of the twentieth century. They demonstrated that high levels of employment and extraordinary sustained growth rates did not require military expenditures. Indeed, their absence may have stimulated growth. Germany and Japan were, and are, a clear rebuttal to the contention that sustained full employment requires defense-stimulated, or war economies. Their prosperity was undoubtedly stimulated by the economic expansion elsewhere, especially in the United States, and that was partly stimulated by armament expenditures and by war. It might thus be argued that indirectly Germany and Japan owed their prosperity to other countries' defense expenditures. However, it is likely that even without defense expenditures, the industrial countries would have had no difficulties in maintaining high levels of employment. More of the civilian demand could have been met, the problem of national economic management made easier, and the competitive market mechanism less injured.

9

Revolution in Government's Role

In recent centuries, with some exceptions, government's role has been limited. Economic activities were essentially the responsibility of private people and private institutions. Even where monarchies or dictatorships prevailed, government was not intended to do what the private sector could do for itself. Government was to protect its people from harm, whether originating within or without the nation, and to provide a mechanism for settling disputes. Governments were ruled by law, and rather severe limits on their powers and functions were regarded as normal. Internationally, there was "anarchy" — commonly described as the law of the jungle — but even in this area custom and habit ruled out certain behavior as barbaric and uncivilized. Respect for law was the keystone: lawbreakers were the pariahs of societies. Governments accepted responsibility for the general welfare but this was narrowly defined, limited to purposes such as police and roads. In the economic field, governments played an important, but limited, role in matters like collecting taxes and protecting domestic industry by tariffs.

This historical role of government began to change in some respects decades before World War II. These changes varied among different countries: the United States had introduced a progressive income tax; in Sweden there was social legislation, and in the U.S.S.R., the Soviet regime. But with World War II the role of government changed drastically everywhere. Government responsibilities and activities expanded hugely; what was regarded as private shrank correspondingly, though private ownership and use of the market mechanism remained important. "Mixed" economies, with large governmental and private sectors, became common. This meant increased powers and authority for government. In many countries governments remain subject to law, but lawmaking by governments is much more extensive and unrestrained. Governments live under the "rules," but hesitate much less to change the rules and make new ones.

The Changed Position of Central Banks

For many decades control of the money supply, including credit, had been a principal form of government intervention in the economic life of the nation. It was far more important than the budget which represented but a small portion of the total national output. By the late nineteenth or early twentieth century, the view was prevalent that government's control of money and credit was supposed to keep the economy running efficiently and enable it to escape avoidable crises resulting from strains in the financing of business activities. Monetary policy, however, was not to alter the fundamental direction of economic life, its structure, or even its pace of growth. This came from the operations of the firms, manufacturers, farmers, bankers, traders, and consumers all working through the market mechanism. Prices, profits, wages were determined by these individuals' economic activities. They made the decisive economic decisions. Because the economic machine, given its complexity, inevitably had frictions, it might need oiling to keep it running smoothly and efficiently, but oil is not gasoline, nor is it the driver or even a regulator. Central banks provided that oil in the form of allowing the banking system to increase or decrease the availability of credit. Troughs in business or trade cycles, when they occurred, could be ameliorated, for example, by provision of credit needed to prevent efficient business firms from going bankrupt. Inefficient firms, however, were not to be supplied with credit; they were allowed to fail even if unemployment resulted directly or indirectly. People accepted such risks as inevitable; many saw them as positive factors that not only made the economy more efficient, but built a sturdy and self-reliant citizenry.

Moreover, the operation of the international gold standard automatically limited the central bank's own freedom of action — a limitation which the central banks themselves usually strongly supported. The gold standard operated not to prevent changes in business conditions or in prices but rather to avoid rigidity in any one direction. It aimed to keep the environment in which firms and consumers made their decisions so as to reward productive efficiency through higher profits and wages and encourage careful consumer decisions via the price mechanism.

Indeed, as a general rule, central banks interfered as little as possible with the market mechanism. However, being

responsible for the supply of money, the central bank became the guardian of the acceptability of and therefore the
value of money — its purchasing power in terms of goods,
both directly at home and indirectly via its exchange value in
currencies abroad. Inflationary price rises reduce the purchasing power of money. Holders of money assets suffer,
while holders of assets like real estate, whose nominal values
tend to rise with — or in advance of — inflation, gain.
Modern central bankers accept the delicate and challenging
task of providing the right amounts of money at the right
time and at the right price (interest rate) to prevent the
sustained price rises which would penalize the very persons
who held assets in forms closely linked to money. Central
bankers everywhere regard the defense of the purchasing
power of their currency as their central ideology. Avoidance of inflation has become a certain sign of success. Those
who do not accept this criterion, be it the government itself,
have found central bankers to be among their principal and
most effective opponents.

Central bankers have understood that, at a given level of
output, increases in money supply make for higher prices —
a simple matter of arithmetic; conversely, less money makes
for lower prices. No one thought that this meant that an
increase or decrease in the money supply would automatically and immediately bring about a corresponding rise or
decline in prices, but it would tend in that direction. The
market mechanism would absorb the increases in money
supply, or adjust to decreases in it, by changing prices,
wages, and profits upward or downward. Consumers remained the decisive element in demand, and competing

private firms the decisive element in supply. Central banks generally retain these preoccupations. Their ideologies have not changed, but under modern conditions, they are unable to conduct monetary affairs in the manner designed to avoid continuing inflation. As governments have extended their own responsibilities and authority, decisions by the central banks have become increasingly dominated by decisions by the government. Governments, not central banks, call the tunc.

The Dominating Role of Government

Government, while it has become very large, does not respond to the same stimuli as the remainder of the economy. Market criteria take on reduced importance in government decision-making, particularly in the choices among expenditures, e.g., roads versus schools. Increased prices for the goods and services required for government may reduce the total in real terms of all goods and services bought by the government, if the budget cannot be increased sufficiently. If the budget can be increased, such higher prices may not decrease the total real government demand at all. In any case, choice is not decided by changes in relative prices. More schools may be built or more armament plant orders placed at the very time when construction costs are rising rapidly; to offset this expenditures on road-building equipment of all kinds may be decreased, even though the prices of these are not rising as rapidly and the need for road-building equipment is unfulfilled. Moreover, government economic decisions are time-consuming to make; too often, the original conditions which prompted the decisions cease to exist, but the process is hard to stop or adapt adequately.

Government's economic decisions are not made solely on economic grounds. Government is not "economic man writ large"; it is "political man writ large," nonetheless making all-important economic decisions and taking all-important economic measures. Everyone wants the government to be "businesslike" — it can try to be honest, careful, nondiscriminatory, fair, and so forth. But it cannot be businesslike! Not only is this "political man writ large" a babe in the woods in making many of these economic decisions, but the psychological incentives and disincentives which explain the behavior of the economic man simply do not exist for him. The criteria for decision-making are necessarily very different.

Again, the development in the new importance of government was far advanced by the end of World War II. Its continuation, too, could readily have been anticipated. However, actual trends have been even more rapid and extensive than expected. Before World War II, particularly before the prewar armament programs of the 1930s, government expenditures were only small proportions of total gross national product. In the United States, for example, government purchases of goods and services in 1929 had amounted to $8.5 billion, about 8 percent of the gross national product. In 1933, the depth of the U.S. depression, they amounted to $8 billion, about 15 percent of the gross national product as the private sector felt the brunt of the depression and thus the government became a larger portion of a shrinking pie. Perhaps even more striking in the light of subsequent developments was that in both these years 75 percent or more of total governmental purchases were made by the state and local authorities; the federal government's expenditures, even in 1933, were less than 4 percent of gross national product. The United States GNP rose to nearly $250 billion by 1950; but government expenditures had risen to some $38 billion, of which nearly 50 percent were federal. Between 1950 and 1970, while GNP in the United States nearly quadrupled, approaching $1000 billion, government expenditures rose more than sixfold — to over $220 billion. Federal expenditures alone reached almost $100 billion. Democratic and Republican administrations both contributed to these trends.

High Taxation and the Taxpayer Revolt

It may be, and is, argued that governments can eliminate the inflationary consequences of their expenditures by exercising their powerful prerogatives to tax more. The proportion of government purchases of goods and services in GNP provides a rather narrow definition of the government's role; as such it does not indicate its full significance. Increases in government expenditures have to be paid for. In most countries, taxation is the principal source of government finance. Indeed, taxes should exceed that portion of the gross national product represented by government purchases of goods and services: tax receipts must cover additional expenditures — payment of interest on the national debt, pensions to veterans, and social security. Taxation, however, is already so high that often consideration of the consequences of taxation is the single most important element in business decision-making.

When economies are expanding rapidly, such tax burdens are somewhat easier to bear. Tax collections tend to rise during expansion even without increases in tax rates. Economic expansion means higher levels of employment and, one would think, a corresponding increase in incomes available to be taxed. But in some industrial countries, full-employment policies have not been accompanied by the expected increases in productivity — increases in output per man.

Even where more satisfactory productivity and output gains have been made, taxation has become a major burden. By now taxes are high in nearly all industrial countries and in many of those in the Third World. Even in countries in which tax revenues are low, measured by actual collections as percentages of national output, high tax rates exist on the statute books.

Funds collected by taxation are only exceptionally available for private investment. Private firms usually finance expansion from retained profits or by borrowing either from banks and other firms or from the capital markets by issuing bonds. Taxes have first claim on the income of the firm — after payments of its debts for labor, rent, supplies, past borrowing, etc. Probably more important, they reduce net earnings and thereby the funds available internally for re-investment. Further, the remaining funds also must be divided between dividends to stockholders and expenditures for investment.

All this seems easier to handle if the firm feels confident

that prices for its output will continue to rise or that bank credit will remain readily available. Again, inflation seems to offer a way out of the firm's thorny difficulties, at least in the short run. Debt becomes more manageable because its nominal (money) amount is fixed as are the interest payments on it. Funds are borrowed in the hope that the future will somehow be different. But repeatedly it proves not to be. In money terms, taxes and costs tend to rise as inflation continues. Borrowing for investment may well prove very wise, but the persistent inflation also creates elements of uncertainty and continuous harassment. In the end, the firm, beset by tax and other difficulties, may simply be forced to sell out to someone who can carry on this process more successfully. Larger firms, or groups of firms, usually have correspondingly larger borrowing capacities, as well as possibilities of economies from the scale or diversification of their activities. Persistent inflation fosters monopolistic and conglomerative tendencies. Some firms may find it relatively easy to pay higher taxes as prices and their incomes rise, but for many firms the inflationary consequences spell defeat.

Taxation fosters other tendencies as well: people everywhere avoid high taxation through legal loopholes, many illegally evade taxation. This disease is not national — but world-wide. It encourages disrespect for law and scorn for strict codes of moral behavior in dealing with government.

Nor is the consumer immune from high taxation. Most directly, increased taxes and costs of borrowing may force some producers out of business and hence reduce employment and income of consumers. Less directly, but quite as important, producers may pass on tax increases in higher prices. The purchasing power of income declines. Unless consumers can get their earnings to rise fast enough by accelerating demands for wage increases or can borrow enough, their real standard of living will commensurately decline. Expectation of rising prices encourages such borrowing and facilitates the granting of wage increases. But such actions, if successful, may nullify one of the principal intended effects of the rising taxes; they do not reduce private consumption to make room for more public expenditures.

Government Financing by Borrowing

Moreover, when, as is quite frequent, governments run budget deficits or themselves must repay debt, they need to borrow for their own purposes. If they borrow from the capital market where the savings of the community are mobilized, they compete with the private sector for funds. Until 1951, the U.S. government's economic policy had, in part, been directed toward minimizing the cost of its own huge war debt. The Federal Reserve, acting as fiscal agent for the government, had to maintain interest rates at the low level of 2 percent. Fiscal policy under these circumstances was *the* instrument of government economic intervention; monetary policy merely implemented it, irrespective of the consequences for the supply of money and credit and the resulting effect on prices. Low interest rates were required by this "fiscal" approach, even if in consequence banks could not assist in increasing savings by offering higher rates of interest on savings deposits or by selling government bonds at rates of interest attractive to investors. Both government and private borrowers could benefit from the low interest rates. Not surprisingly, the demand for bank credit increased. The shortfall between the amounts people wished to save and the amounts they wished to borrow grew. Money creation by the banking system could finance the difference; yet money creation might push demand for goods beyond available supplies, establishing an inflationary equilibrium between supply and demand.

The "Accord of 1951" between the U.S. Treasury and the Federal Reserve represented a dramatic shift in economic policy. It restored the Federal Reserve's traditional powers to alter interest rates and control the money supply through adjustments in reserve requirements and open-market operations of buying and selling government bonds. The accord itself reflected nascent concerns both with inflation's deleterious effects and with the capacity of fiscal policy, largely alone, to combat them. By the 1950s the problem was quite generally recognized, not only in North America but in Europe as well. Monetary policy, therefore, recovered a good deal of its historic flexibility. Central banks again became important instruments of national economic management, although no longer independent. Moreover, they operated in a very different world dedicated to the new role of government.

Monetary policy still tended to be "cautious." It avoided incurring public and political wrath by placing less emphasis on "old-fashioned" concerns: inflation, the purchasing power of money, and the competitiveness of the economy. It focused, instead, on employment. Although monetary policy became a "fine tuner" in managing the economy, the fiscal activities of the government remain the principal influence on economic behavior.

Moreover, the effective use of interest-rate policy to induce more savings and reduce effective demand was bedeviled by the by-products of high taxation and other prevailing fiscal practices. High taxation, as we have seen, could be offset by increased borrowing encouraged by an inflationary environment in which incurring debt was less worrisome. High interest rates might normally be expected to reduce borrowing. However, interest paid on loans is tax-deductible. In the United States, for example, for the firm or person paying marginal tax rates in the neighborhood of 30 to 50 percent (not at all unusual), an interest rate of 8 percent is equivalent after taxes to one of 4 to 6 percent. Further, if prices were rising at, say, 3 or 4 percent per year, the interest paid by the firm or individual after tax might be largely offset by the price rise. If price rises of these magnitudes were reasonably to be expected, "rational" businessmen and consumers would not, and indeed do not, hesitate to borrow even at interest rates of 8 percent or higher. What seem like fantastically high interest charges by past experience would be required to induce businessmen (or consumers) to reduce borrowing and thus expenditure. Yet interest rates of these magnitudes were regarded as extraordinarily high in many countries, and monetary authorities in these countries hesitated to even urge, much less impose them.

Today investors may find themselves paying higher interest rates because of government competition for money.

Government's ability to pay higher interest rates is not limited, as is that of a private borrower. Even if interest rates are pushed up by government borrowing, the government cannot refrain from borrowing to meet expenditures that have been already legislated and authorized. The government must pay its bills. Higher interest rates can, however, discourage private investment, particularly in sectors where output prices or capital values are not rising as fast as the inflation. The cost of bank loans can be raised to a level too high to make such private borrowing economically feasible even though interest payments are tax deductible. Under these circumstances the government, in effect, restricts private borrowing to make room for itself.

Thus, the government appears on one level to have recognized its own power to encourage or discourage private activity. On another, it has often failed either to recognize the magnitude of that power and its pervasive impact on the economy, or to exercise that power by criteria of economic management. Fiscal measures — taxation and borrowing — tend to be inadequate or excessive and ill-tuned; they become a series of shocks to which economies must try to adjust. The idea that fiscal policy, by and large, can handle the problem of business fluctuations by minimizing their size or duration — particularly by ensuring that downswings do not go too far or last too long — remains essentially sound; in practice, however, governments do not behave efficiently. Poor timing and inappropriateness of action simply happen too often everywhere.

10

Inflation, Prosperity, and Depression

The Coexistence of Inflation and Prosperity

In a noninflationary environment, tax increases and government borrowing from the public might generally be expected to reduce consumption expenditures, making room for private and social investment. Yet the same instruments can have perverse effects in an environment of rising prices — particularly if government activity is large and rapidly growing. To the extent this is so, in the United States, the United Kingdom, and elsewhere, an extraordinary situation arises. Increased taxation, normally one of the most potent weapons in restraining the economy, can accelerate the inflationary process. National economic management is thereby importantly changed and weakened. This may help explain why inflation has proved so intractable. If so, this is a direct consequence of the fact that governments have not learned as yet how to fulfill their responsibilities without creating inflation. They continue to rely on mechanisms which were effective in periods when their role in economic life was much less important.

Inflation as a Global Phenomenon

Were the phenomena of the postwar period found in only one country their implications would be much less. One country experiencing inflationary pressures, or the shortages created by excessive demand, could find some means of importing more from abroad. By doing so, its own shortages and inflationary pressures would diminish. Countries not undergoing such pressures might well be willing to provide credits to enable the afflicted country to import more because the credit-extending country would thereby be promoting its own exports. In this way, the country with inflation would obtain some, if not entirely sufficient, relief by taking advantage of the productive capacity in other countries.

The situation we face, however, is dramatically different. The shortage of goods relative to the demand for them is a global phenomenon. "Overheated" economies, where the persistent underlying trend is for demand to exceed available supply pushing up prices and costs, simply cannot find sufficient idle capacity elsewhere to increase output enough to offset their own inadequacy of supplies. If this happens in a particular commodity, the total impact is small. But overheated economies cannot find idle capacity elsewhere because so many economies are simultaneously overheated.

Moreover, overheated economies are usually less eager to provide export credits and international development assistance. For developing countries this severely limits their ability to import more to augment domestic supplies — a direct help to reducing inflationary pressures.

Expectations of continuing rises in prices and costs have spread from country to country. By the end of the 1960s, this development was clearly world-wide. People everywhere had come to judge it most likely that prices, costs, and money incomes would continue to rise in the foreseeable future even during periods of recession — and might well do so at accelerating rates. This was a sharp change in expectations from previous decades, one that completely altered the world's economic and social environment. Even if prices were to level off in most countries for the remainder of the century, the price increases already experienced greatly exceed those of any century in recorded European and American economic history.

Continental Europe encountered quite serious inflation immediately after World War II. Inflation in postwar Europe was generally handled with skill and courage and, perhaps more important, it left behind a legacy of financial leaders more sensitive to the problem of inflation, a sensitivity shared by only a few in the United States. Yet that inflation was mild by comparison to what Germany had undergone after the First World War. Then prices had skyrocketed so rapidly that wages and prices of goods could not be fixed — even for a day. By contrast, even the very high rates of inflation in countries like Brazil and Chile in the 1950s, i.e., 50 percent per year, seem much milder. The Third World, however, had more cases of "serious" inflation than the developed countries, that is, higher annual rates of price increases. These events fostered a widespread misconception: inflation was not a serious enduring problem for the industrial world. There, there was no danger of "runaway" inflation, just "runaway" deflation — severe and prolonged unemployment. This despite the fact that in the postwar period virtually no country, developed or developing, has experienced for any appreciable length of time the declining prices which would have been the prewar expectation even during periods of prosperity. There were some periods when prices rose faster than in others — as during the Korean war. Even though prices reached new heights at that time, the end of that war did not bring a lowering of the average level of consumer prices. The rate of inflation was higher in the 1960s than it had been in the 1950s.

Twenty years of rising prices should logically have had at least one result: recognition that the world is in a unique period of continuing universal inflation. But, after decades, this realization is shared by few. People are well aware of the inflation in their own countries; they are not yet aware of its persistency and durability, its strength and severity, nor of its world-wide character. They need to understand that prices will trend only upward in the foreseeable future unless governmental policies change markedly to alter social and political behavior as well as economic. Until this happens, some combinations of government policies and other circumstances, though not involving major change, might reduce the rate of increase in the cost of living, or even induce a short-lived leveling off of prices — but only temporarily.

Continued inflation in one's country has been the only reasonable assumption for any long-run purpose. The prudent man during the last three decades has been the one who has bet on persistent inflation. Will this be even more true of the 1970s?

Is Inflation Any Country's Fault?

Some argue that the United States is the single most important cause of world-wide inflation. But this is not, as is widely believed, primarily because the United States' balance-of-payments deficit has flooded the world with allegedly unwanted dollars, thereby spreading inflation. In a different world, the "flood" of dollars might have been more universally welcomed as facilitating domestic policies to achieve higher levels of income and expenditure without fear of the balance-of-payments constraint. Even in the world as it is today, lower-income countries in need of foreign exchange to help finance development welcome the flood of dollars; they regret only that most of it has gone to the industrialized nations.

Understandably, in view of their own inflationary conditions, industrialized countries have tended to look askance at the additional expansionary forces coming from abroad, particularly when the source is an entity as large as the United States.

But it is the fundamental domestic causes of inflation — the enduring changes in demand, supply, and market conditions — that all countries must recognize if they are to cope successfully with inflationary problems. Without the widespread prevalence of these conditions, particularly in the major industrial countries, the international transmission of persistent inflation would be of minor importance. The "Americanization" of consumption and production everywhere may well be a more important factor than the U.S. balance of payments in explaining the inflationary situation of the modern world.

U.S. prosperity, of course, also played a significant role in helping other countries to increase their output capacity. This process has, however, been more than offset by the increased demands. I hasten to add that U.S. stagnation or sustained depression would also have been disastrous for other countries. It would have probably eliminated world-wide persistent inflation, but at a huge cost in unemployment and lost output. The way to tackle the pernicious effects of inflation cannot be to substitute economic stagnation and serious prolonged unemployment for persistent inflation. The only practical way is to eliminate the persistent infla-tion and this requires recognition that persistent inflation is not only not needed, but is a handicap in pursuing employ-ment, growth, and income distribution objectives.

The Coexistence of Inflation and Unemployment:
The Latest Phase

In 1971 and 1972, there has been relative recession in Europe, North America, and, to some extent, even in Japan. They have interacted. Each has impeded the others' process of recovery and prolonged the period of recession. Cyclical recessions do occur. This one had the common characteristic of combining relatively high levels of unemployment (high by postwar standards) in the developed countries and rap-idly rising prices — the fruit of decades of economic mis-management. The fundamental lesson to be learned from this cyclical recession is the need to deal efficiently with persistent inflation.

This failure to deal with persistent inflation is not only

America's; it is well-nigh universal. Symptoms have been mistaken for causes. Remedies have been applied only to the symptoms. Aspirin may suppress a fever, but if the fever is symptomatic of a fundamental illness, suppression of the symptoms and postponement of therapy only mean more difficulties and less likelihood of success in coping with the illness. Policies which attack the symptoms of inflation, not its causes, only postpone sustained recovery of output, employment, and productivity. They allow inflation to become even more entrenched and ensure re-emergence of price rises in even larger magnitudes than before. As such they are doomed to failure.

Inflationary expectations are not new, though in the United States it is still fashionable to date existing inflation from the latter part of the 1960s. Consumers and producers acted with awareness of inflationary expectations long before experts and political leaders formally acknowledged their presence. Even now, its true strength and influence are not recognized because of the failure to see inflation as a long-lived and enduring phenomenon rather than one that is transitory and of recent vintage. Political leaders have been reluctant to admit the strength of these inflationary expectations. Experts could not agree on whether continuing price increases were or were not, on balance, desirable. Nor had they suggested any politically acceptable remedies. It is not that political leaders defended inflation. Rather they failed to act effectively — often for obvious political reasons. In developing countries, many have erroneously seen inflation as a means of encouraging investment, innovation, and increased employment while bringing about needed social

mobility. Those who regarded the existing social and economic institutions as inadequate, rigid, and resistant to change
through ordinary means, saw the effects of inflation as
desirable. Their hopes were to prove illusory.

There has, in the postwar period, never been any question
that the target of maintaining "full" employment has priority
over that of controlling inflation. Few believed with confidence that the three objectives — avoidance of unacceptable
unemployment rates, achievement of reasonable growth
rates, and of monetary stability — could simultaneously be
realized. Lip service was paid to this. The words of some
even indicated a belief that it could be done; but actions
usually belied the words. And many still view the advocacy
of anti-inflationary priorities as tantamount to advocating
prolonged and wasteful, if not severe, unemployment. By
1968–69, it had become fashionable to recognize inflation
as a serious problem in the United States as well as elsewhere,
though not much was done about it. The adoption of the
New Economic Policy in August 1971 indicated that the
U.S. Administration saw the need for doing something about
inflation. The measures taken were rather drastic, but they
may prove to be fundamentally wrong if the problem has not
been seen in historical perspective and the strength of inflationary expectations are therefore underestimated. Until the
strength and persistency of inflation are more realistically
evaluated, and — equally important — until its corrosive
effects on all aspects of existence are more fully appreciated
by the public at large, effective government measures cannot
be expected.

Conditions of societies remain "tolerable" for considerable

numbers during periods of temporary inflation. But when inflation persists long enough it becomes increasingly intolerable for greater numbers. The fabric of society is eroded and the human costs become incalculable. The solution of other problems like pollution and hard-core unemployment may then become impossible — economically, socially, and politically.

I believe we are entering a period in which the pace of persistent inflation will become so disruptive as to force its recognition and solution. Persistent inflation is not the oil, it is the grit in the machinery we call society. It threatens, sooner or later, to bring the machinery to a halt. It cannot be expected to be self-correcting, like temporary inflation. The existing backlog of private and public demands plus the never-ending process of creating major new demands in modern societies mean that the long-run problem will remain one of inadequate output, not inadequate demand.

IV

A Closer Look at the World
of Persistent Inflation:
Economic Signs and Effects

11

Prices and Expectations

Signs, Causes, Effects

Changes in the more traditional indicators of inflation —
rates of change in prices, wages, and money supply — can
be regarded as signs, causes, or effects of inflation. Wage
increases can be a sign of inflation: they are one of many
prices undergoing sustained increases. They can also be a
cause of inflation: they add to producers' costs and may then
be incorporated in higher prices to consumers. They can be
an effect of inflation: the demand for a rise in wages may be a
consequence of the rise in the cost of living. Similarly, a
rapid expansion in the money supply can be evidence of
inflation. At the same time, it can be a primary cause of
inflation: too much lubrication eliminates the minimal friction needed to keep the economic machine from runaway
speeds. Or the increase in money supply may be an effect:
the money supplied is needed to finance the higher nominal
level of transactions.

That most signs of inflation may likewise be cause or
effect reflects, in part, the highly complex nature of modern
economies and lends great operational importance to careful

analysis of prevailing conditions. In tackling persistent inflation, an over simplified view may lead to wrong decisions by
private individuals and firms, as well as by governments. It is
easy to go wrong by assuming that inflation results from
excessive wage increases, or from budgetary deficits, or from
too much expansion of the money supply. But there is no
escape — either from analysis of the complexities, or from
the need to make decisions. And complex situations are difficult to analyze and judge. Moreover, the policy measures to
correct them may need to be multifaceted and therefore hard
to put together, get adopted and implemented.

Prices

The most familiar single indicator in inflation is the change
in the average or general price level. Such changes may be
sporadic and very short-lived with no pattern; they may be
"seasonal," reflecting a range of things from crop cycles to
Christmas trees; they may be "cyclical," following the peak-
trough patterns of business "cycles." Yet others, and these
are our primary concern, are longer-run trends extending
over a number of years.

Changes in consumer prices are measured by changes in
the average price paid by consumers for all goods and services taken together. These are expressed, for convenience,
in statistical indexes — a consumer price, cost of living, or
retail price index. In constructing these indexes, recognition
or "weight" is given to the relative importance of different
goods and services to the "average" consumer. All consumers differ, of course, in what they buy, but in order to
follow and analyze what is happening, an "average" or typi-

cal consumer is taken to represent all consumers. Such simplification, necessary and useful as it is, is frequently mystifying. Most people find that their own experience is very different from what is expressed in these indexes. Moreover, the index is often the average of an entire country, even though consumer prices may differ markedly in various regions within the country. Perhaps even worse, this "average" may be for only one or two cities because data for other areas are not available, yet it is used to represent the entire country.

Disguised price rises, not reflected in the price index, are a particularly vital part of understanding what inflation and faulty methods of dealing with it mean for lower and middle income groups — a majority of the population. In some countries, some prices (like rent or public utilities) are fixed by law or public bodies, or subsidized to the consumer. Such items are usually included in the price indexes at the official prices — even if black markets in which buying and selling takes place at much higher prices exist and such transactions account for a large part of the consumption. In other cases, products may shrink in size, deteriorate in quality, or become less available, forcing consumers to buy increased quantities of more expensive substitutes. All have seen the phenomenon of the vanishing candy bar, which goes up in price and simultaneously becomes smaller in size. The inexpensive toy, like the inexpensive apartment or house, is either not obtainable or unbelievably poor in quality. In still other cases, part of the increased price is measured in time. The adage that "time is money" becomes ever more meaningful as consumers spend hours searching for lower-priced items, or wait months for an electrician. Such delays are increasingly common. But none of these is easily captured in a statistical index.

It is also not uncommon to find that certain items rapidly rising in price carry little weight in the index. This is particularly true of better-quality consumption goods. Prices may therefore rise more rapidly than the average for people with higher incomes, who tend to purchase such products and services. On the other hand, as these prices rise, they simply force lower and middle income groups to eliminate or reduce better-quality purchases in their total consumption; in this way their actual consumption has been sharply affected, although their "average" price level may seem to rise less than that of those able to buy the more expensive goods.

Controlled rents provide another kind of example. They may hold down the average price level. But the condition of the poorer, often deplorably run-down housing obtained for controlled prices is not reflected in price indexes. "Beneficiaries" of rent control may suffer a marked reduction in housing consumption without a corresponding reduction in rent. But this is a hidden rent increase. Similarly, interest rates for consumer credit in a price index understate the inflation for those unable to obtain consumer credit on "usual" terms. Poorer groups are much more likely to have to pay interest rates verging on — if not surpassing — extortion, plus exorbitant penalties for delayed payments. Moreover, the ability to deduct interest payments from income tax is much less significant for lower income groups.

The indexes of prices in controlled economies are not comparable with those in mixed economies. In the controlled economies, failure to reflect changes in quality as well as availability of goods can be even more important weaknesses of price indexes than elsewhere. In Soviet-type economies, persistent inflation is seen more in nonprice indicators: shortages of supply, narrow range of choices, poorer quality, and delays in delivery.

With these caveats in mind, let's look at the cost-of-living indexes for some countries: During the 1950s and 1960s, using 15 industrialized countries as a sample, about half of them experienced cost-of-living rises of less than 3 percent per year and the other half higher, Japan being the highest with an average rise of over 8 percent per year in the 1950s and about 10 percent in the 1960s. This may not seem particularly high. What is often neglected is that price rises have been continuous and therefore cumulative in their effect. Moreover, they have tended to accelerate even in the industrial countries. Under these circumstances, as individual prices rise, other prices are inevitably pulled up. There were virtually no cases of countries experiencing price declines from one year to another and, for most countries, the rate of inflation was higher in the 1960s and early 1970s than in the 1950s as inflationary expectations gathered strength and momentum.

The disruptive effects of inflationary expectations might be regarded as minimal, say, if the public could expect more or less regular price rises of 1 percent or more. Over time, even this requires major adjustments, since only 1 percent a year cumulates in 30 years to nearly 35 percent increase and, in 50 years, to nearly 65 percent. These time spans are well within modern man's purview — within his calculations concerning housing, children's education, pensions, or estate planning.

In practice, however, inflationary expectations of 1 percent or so set the stage for higher rates of persistent inflation; they lead repeatedly to redefinitions of "acceptable" rates of persistent inflation. This has already happened in a number of industrialized countries in the postwar period: acceptable rates have climbed from 1 percent to 2, 3, to 5 or 6 percent, or even more. In industrialized societies the eventual disruption, or at least very serious disturbances of the economy and the entire society can be experienced at rates of increases much closer to what is now considered "normal" by many — say 2 to 4 percent per year. In 1972, the United Kingdom is experiencing inflation of 10 percent after a long period of much lower annual rates of price increases. The United States was officially defining as acceptable inflation price increases of 2 to 3 percent per year, while some experts were even speaking of 5 to 6 percent per year as acceptable. Rates of 10 percent and more per annum are viewed with equanimity in a number of less developed countries — Korea, not to mention again old veterans of persistent inflation like Chile.

To take the argument a step further, imagine the U.S. or Canada, or Japan, or Western Europe experiencing 15 to 50 percent inflation per year — rates experienced in the Third World. If they did, such countries would be even more rapidly and profoundly shaken than the Third World countries where persistent inflation has brought with it continuous political and social disorder, disrupting and destroying, among other things, the environment necessary for sustained social and economic progress.

12

Money Illusions and Effects

Money Illusions

Experience with inflation after World War II points to another hard, stubborn fact: to many people, ever fewer but still many, rising prices and rising money incomes remain synonymous with prosperity. In fact, increases in national output and incomes may be largely "nominal," that is, measured in money, rather than in goods and services actually produced and consumed. Nonetheless, money illusions are not recognized for what they are. "Money illusions" here encompass the general point in which people are overly impressed by *money* income, value, costs, and so forth; they are therefore deflected from examining other aspects.

An individual firm may find it quite agreeable to live in an environment of rising prices and wages if it is compatible with high levels of usage of plant and equipment and reasonable profits. What is good for the individual firms is generalized as being good for the entire nation — or even the international community. Thus, in many countries, particularly when production and incomes are rising faster than elsewhere, the fact that rapidly rising prices can endanger the continuation of upward trends is lost in the exuberance of a Wild West "let-'er-rip" spirit. Countries throughout the world have repeatedly undergone such phases. They seem to hope in each separate instance that, this time, unlike the last, persistent inflation will not disrupt the progress being made.

The money illusion affects the attitude toward giving and accepting bank credit. If inflation is at 5 percent per year, a borrower paying 8 percent interest per year (the nominal rate) can service his debt if he uses the credit to yield a "real" return of less than 3 percent, the "real" rate of interest. In addition, inflation is likely, by itself, to bring him additional money income. People have continued to talk of interest rates as high, unacceptably high, even though the continuing rises in prices meant that borrowers would have no difficulty in paying much higher rates. In fact, credit has been unbelievably cheap. Although interest rates paid by borrowers virtually everywhere are much higher than before World War II, they are much less effective in restraining the demand for credit because the declining prewar price trend has been replaced by the rising postwar trend — interest is paid in money of steadily decreasing purchasing power and loans are taken on the assumption that this will continue to be so.

Banks observe that inefficient firms survive in inflation, perhaps not as well as efficient firms, but well enough to pay interest on loans. Thus the amount of the loan principal becomes relatively less significant as the inflation greatly increases money earnings, and loan repayments remain fixed. Even if repayment requires new borrowing, the burden of the new loans also erodes as the inflation continues. Banks can be less cautious in extending loans. Firms can look with equanimity on increasing costs, including wages and interest, as bank credit will help finance such difficulties.

A more subtle manifestation of the "money illusion" is the eagerness with which people welcome devices designed to make inflation more tolerable but do not attack its underlying causes or eliminate its effects. Thus, devaluation of the currency of the inflating economy by changing the foreign-exchange rate makes inflation more tolerable because exports remain internationally competitive. Such economies are often thought "successful." They are, indeed, successful in that without devaluation the country could well experience overwhelming balance-of-payments deficits. With devaluation, foreign-exchange expenditures can be made to equal foreign-exchange receipts; the external books are balanced. With continuing inflation, however, devaluation will prove only temporarily effective; the domestic situation, employment, output, and price, may become even worse; the devaluation will have to be repeated, or the exchange rates will have to be set free to float or fluctuate. The balance-of-payments deficit then disappears, but the other harmful effects of inflation remain.

Cost-of-living adjustment clauses in wage contracts do make inflation more tolerable, at least for those who get sufficient adjustments to offset price increases. These clauses may weaken demands for wage increases larger than the cost-of-living increases, particularly when they also include allowances for increased labor productivity. All these ameliorate the effects of inflation. They may well give the impression that incomes in general are being defended from erosion of their purchasing power and weaken public demand to end the inflation. Thus, they may actually help perpetuate the inflationary pressures. In fact, though theoretically all incomes could thereby be defended in the narrow sense, the incomes of only a few are fully protected by such cost-of-living clauses; most are not.

Cost-of-living allowances not only reduce the number who are interested in effective anti-inflationary policies, but because they perpetuate acceptance of inflation, they strengthen inflationary expectations — the most intractable element in modern inflation. They illustrate the vicious circularity of the inflation phenomenon. As long as inflation is deemed likely to continue, it is impossible to oppose cost-of-living adjustments. Those who do not have them are deprived of one way of defending themselves against inflation; they are forced to seek and adopt other ways — like much larger wage demands. The allowances, however, are unlikely to disappear until the inflation itself has ended and inflationary expectations have greatly weakened, if not disappeared. At the same time, the existence of inflation with its accompaniment of high business costs and high levels of government expenditures, taxes, and deficits creates strong pressures against generalizing cost-of-living allowances or having them keep pace with the actual increase in living costs.

Destruction of Illusions

Matured inflationary expectations lead to a deeper understanding of the "money illusion." This new understanding itself weakens and eventually destroys the "money illusion." Inflation often takes root in the soil of the belief that rising prices and wages accompanied by increasing money supply are harbingers of prosperity. It grows on the defensive measures people — individuals and firms — use to protect themselves against its effects. These defensive measures nurture and strengthen the inflation and transform the public attitude from viewing inflation as temporary and short-lived to something enduring. Inflationary expectations then bloom. They are the outgrowth of a process extending over years.

Confidence in the national currency is a sturdy plant. Nearly all countries have enjoyed the benefits of this confidence in the past. With little watering, this confidence sends up new shoots even after a number of years of continuous price rises. That confidence may well prove more lasting and more resilient than the facts warrant. Inflation lasting even some years may go virtually ignored.

But once inflationary expectations become strong, the public disposition alters radically. Measures to restore price stability (usually called stabilization measures), even mild ones, meet a hardening skepticism instead of a quick revival of traditional attitudes of confidence. The very stabilization measures are often taken as confirmation that things are going badly, further diminishing any confidence that may remain.

The experience of the last two or three decades has taught that loss of confidence in national currencies results not only from extraordinary events, like war destruction, or political or social revolution, but can be the silent, largely ignored, and perhaps even more enduring consequence of years of persistent inflation. Confidence in the national currency weakens reluctantly, but when it does, a major corrosive factor has entered the life of the country. A critical element of national cohesion and an instrument for facilitating community living becomes enfeebled. Modern societies, already trying to cope with deep feelings of drift, inadequacy, and alienation, lose a vital stabilizing element. This nurtures the seeds of friction, instability, and disruption.

Inflationary expectations become the frame of reference both for private decisions of consumption and investment and for public decisions on expenditures and revenues. By acting "as if" inflation will continue, people virtually assure that it will; the likelihood of price declines weakens steadily: the prophecy is fulfilled.

Speculation, Hedging, and the Flight of Money

During inflation, activities increase markedly which satisfy the combined desires of taking advantage of the opportunities for extraordinary profits that arise in inflation and protecting income, accumulated assets, or savings from the eroding effects of inflation. The balance of emphasis between these desires, however, changes importantly as a country moves from temporary inflation — a short-lived rise in prices — into persistent inflation.

In fact, different people and firms are in simultaneously different stages of this process — some come more quickly to a psychological set of inflationary expectations than others. While all will not behave uniformly, the underlying patterns do exist. These can be most helpful in judging the character of the problems of inflation and alternative approaches to them.

During short-lived inflations, concern tends to center on protecting the purchasing power of current incomes and, if possible, a few may seek profit from the special opportunities for gain. At that time, a wage increase which keeps up with, or close to, price rises is quite satisfactory. Accumulated savings can be left more or less intact. A "flyer" in a real estate venture, if it can be financed and is not too risky, is attractive. "Blue chip" stocks are particularly attractive, combining some hope for rise in value with relatively little risk and the likelihood of steady, possibly increasing, dividends.

As inflation continues, attention shifts more toward protection of accumulated savings. Prices are no longer expected to return to levels that restore the purchasing power. Quite the contrary!

Persistent inflation, as seen in the period since World War II, has been characterized by unusually high rates of interest, particularly on long-term bonds. Why lock up your money in long-term bonds unless the earnings are quite certain at least to offset the decline in purchasing power of the funds invested? Long-term interest rates, even for highly rated borrowers, have assumed levels nearly twice as high as those of the prewar period.

Persistent inflation is also generally characterized by increased speculative activities: in land, in buildings, in goods, and foreign exchange. Speculation, induced by continued inflation, only feeds the fires of inflation. Under noninflationary conditions, speculation, in the sense of buying or selling commodities in anticipation of future changes in prices, may help to make market conditions more orderly. Goods are withheld from declining markets in anticipation of reversals in prices, and supplies are increased in rising price markets, again in anticipation of future price reversals. In both cases the speculative activities keep prices from falling or rising too much; they tend to keep prices in equilibrium or at least dampen price fluctuations upward and downward.

Under inflationary conditions, speculation may simply mean withholding goods from markets in anticipation of further price rises, thus increasing the gap between demand and supply. Speculative activities no longer seem as risky against the background of continuing price rises. This is somewhat different from hedging against inflation by seeking and obtaining assets whose nominal or money value is likely to go up with prices; caution causes the hedger to switch out of liquid assets: savings deposits or government and corporate bonds. He thereby maintains the purchasing power of his accumulated savings by putting them into stocks or real property like buildings or land. The "speculator" seeks more than merely to defend the purchasing power of his investment. He may look for assets likely to rise more than the general price level. Alternatively, he may seek business opportunities as "tax havens," minimizing taxes because as money income rises, his marginal tax rates climb to levels he has never experienced before. Or, discouraged by the frequent "stop and go" behavior of an economy experiencing continuous inflation, he may decide to invest elsewhere. Capital flees the country. This happened in France in the chronic inflation years of the 1950s, and repeatedly has plagued other countries — Argentina, Brazil, and Chile — throughout the postwar period.

In countries with sustained inflation, investments in land, particularly in urban properties or in rural areas close to urban centers, become major business activities. Land values can be relied on, as a rule, to rise with or faster than the general price level. With proper selection, land provides particularly attractive opportunities for the speculator. In Tokyo, some residential property is selling for ten thousand times (in money terms) its selling price in 1934; though this is a very exceptional case, others of lesser but still very large magnitudes are commonly found. Closely related is speculation in commercial and luxury apartment buildings. Widespread squalid housing surrounds pockets of beautiful residential areas and handsome, shining new commercial buildings adorn the business section while older buildings are left to fall apart and decay. Visitors to Rio de Janeiro, São Paulo, Acapulco, Mexico City, Beirut, New York, Chicago, Accra, Lahore, and London have seen evidence of this phenomenon.

Inflation seems to make businessmen interested in buying and selling commodities rather than in manufacturing them. A marvelous example of what can happen during persistent inflation is that of a large commercial building block in London. Huge and attractive, the block has been ready for occupancy for years, but empty! The owners, whatever their reasons, can afford to have it empty because its capital value is rising very rapidly. Like Mark Twain's sack of flour in a Western frontier mining community with scarce supplies and ample money, which was sold over and over again, but never consumed; so much more could be made in buying and selling the scarce flour than in using it to make bread.

Uncertainty about future prices creates opportunities for extraordinary profits for those who guess correctly. Increasing numbers are prepared to back their skill and luck against others' in guessing how future prices will behave. The game is no longer played mainly by experts. Confident or hopeful novices eagerly join in; slot machines are small stuff and poker takes skill. The economy becomes a huge roulette wheel. Indeed, one of the unquantifiable but surely more costly aspects of inflation is the loss of entrepreneurial skill and imagination to speculative activities at home and abroad.

Governmental controls over the purchase of foreign exchange to make payments abroad provide special opportunities for speculation. Governments impose such controls because the expected demand for foreign exchange is thought to exceed its expected availability. This difference could be eliminated and equilibrium achieved by using the exchange-rate mechanism. Frequently, however, the country is unwilling to devalue its currency, despite continuous domestic inflation at rates higher than those in other countries. Foreign-exchange supplies therefore need to be rationed according to some system of priorities. Import or foreign-exchange licenses granted by the government authorities became valuable properties. They entitle the holder to obtain scarce goods or services which command premium prices in the domestic market. A market arises in the exchange licenses themselves. Profits are sought not from importing of goods, but from exploiting the ability, legally or otherwise, to obtain these licenses. Inflation turns productive and sound businessmen into foreign-exchange speculators. This happens so often that it is tempting to declare it an axiom of human behavior. When persistent inflation does not exist, this situation, if it occurs at all, is likely to be of minor significance.

Like domestic controls, foreign-exchange controls go beyond straining the administrative capacities of government. Too often they overtax the ability of government officials to resist temptation: in the end, they place their private gain ahead of public morality. This is not the petty larceny found here and there in all governments. It is huge, pervasive, and continuous corruption. Corruption has gone so far in a number of countries as to become a major source of political instability. Nor have such scandals plagued only the less developed countries; industrialized countries have also suffered from such ills when unrealistic economic management has resulted in persistent inflation and unrealistic controls were imposed to cope with its effects. Look at the sad history of rent controls.

13

Unemployment and Price Controls

Unemployment and Capacity Utilization

In the pre–World War II years, employment, output, and prices went down together and rose together. After World War II this pattern of behavior was drastically altered. When employment fell, the *rate of increase* of prices sometimes fell, but prices continued to rise. The forces generating continued price rises, particularly inflationary expectations, remained strong, though demand in the economy might be temporarily insufficient to achieve "full" employment. Since World War II, it has proved virtually impossible in the industrialized countries to achieve very low unemployment (as currently and popularly defined) and very high plant utilization without inflation. Many take this to indicate that the two are incompatible. Many accept the converse: inflation can be avoided only by accepting higher levels of unemployment and lower levels of plant utilization. The statistics alone may seem to warrant this conclusion. This does not prove, however, the inevitability of the relation.

Until we do learn how to break this relationship, declining

levels of unemployment in industrialized countries do warn that inflationary pressures are probably building up — even if they do not materialize quickly. As this lesson is repeated, consumers and producers translate into heightened inflationary expectations the knowledge that unemployment is approaching levels which in the past have resulted in accelerating price and wage increases. No longer are they guided by price and wage behavior alone; they view changes in employment as precursors to price and wage changes.

In a sense, governments, too, can use this relation as an "early warning" of strengthening inflationary trends. Unfortunately, forewarned is not necessarily forearmed. Governments understandably cheer the news of reaching very low levels of unemployment, despite the repeated experience of consequent inflation; they have no programs for maintaining satisfactory levels of unemployment that simultaneously avoid inflation. This is so even where historical experience has repeatedly been the consequent strengthening of inflation accompanying the recovery in employment; governments then have been forced to adopt policies which give rise to unacceptably large unemployment. This is sometimes rationalized as solving one problem at a time, a sensible attitude if unavoidable and if workable — but only then. So far, it has been notoriously unsuccessful and might very well be avoidable.

But caution is needed here. What are "very low" rates of unemployment and "high" levels of plant utilization? In one sense these seem fairly obvious ideas. Plant utilization is most often judged by historical standards: a comparison with what is "typical" under particular conditions. Very low levels of unemployment to a North American mean that the official index of unemployed is about 4 percent or less; in the United Kingdom and Germany, the term "full employment" means more like 1 or 2 percent unemployed. The higher U.S. figure is partly due to the fact that hard-core or structural unemployment is relatively more prevalent there than in other industrial countries and partly because the technical definitions of unemployment differ.

The "hard-core" unemployed are, for the most part, people in situations which make it very difficult to place them in vacancies somewhere in the economy. This category changes over time and varies from country to country. In the United States, young black people in cities are an outstanding example. Family conditions, lack of skills and schooling, inadequate transportation, poor health, discriminatory racial practices have made it much more difficult for them to find employment. Very high rates of unemployment can exist among the hard-core — even when the economy as a whole enjoys full employment; large numbers of vacancies coexist with large numbers of unemployed.

These "economic" figures are, thus, to a large extent politically and socially determined. They reflect public attitudes and political realities that are culturally induced; they are not dictated by some objective necessities or external forces. This does not make them less valid. But it does suggest that they are not immutable, though changing them involves strongly held societal attitudes not easily altered by "objective" arguments, or automatically changed by variations in objective economic conditions.

Regardless of how unemployment is defined, it is an average figure; it disguises great differences among sectors of the population — rural vs. urban; women vs. men; younger vs. older; skilled vs. unskilled; trade unionists vs. unorganized labor; educated vs. uneducated. This is also sometimes seen geographically. In the United Kingdom, while areas near London had more vacancies than people looking for jobs, serious unemployment existed in parts of Wales, Scotland, and northwestern England, and even more serious unemployment was chronic in Northern Ireland. Critical labor shortages may push up wages; or a shortage of certain critical commodities, coupled with strong demand for labor to produce them, may push up both wages and prices in that activity, while elsewhere people and plants remain idle. How odd it seems, particularly to dwellers in suburbia of industrialized countries that it takes days, if not weeks, to get a plumber, painter, electrician, carpenter, or gardener, while newspapers report "unacceptable" levels of unemployment. In the Caribbean countries sugar production is held back by lack of sugarcane cutters, yet unemployment rates in these countries remain very high. At the same time, wage increases tend to spread throughout the economy despite the existence of unemployment.

Such paradoxes present one of the sharpest challenges to successful management of our economies and societies. The economy experiences inflationary consequences from its attempts, whether by increased government expenditures or encouraged private activity, to push demand to the very high levels where it will cause all labor to be absorbed, despite the new difficulties it is likely to face. Special problems are not tackled vigorously because of the hope and expectation that the general increase in demand will provide the solution to the special problems. But it does not. The special problems remain unsolved. If governments tackle the special problems of structural or hard-core unemployment, as supplementary to policies to augment general demand, the combined efforts are likely to create even more excessive demand and inflation. Frequently, then, governments cut back or eliminate measures specially targeted to deal with hard-core unemployment. High levels of unemployment continue, while inflation is strengthened by the efforts to increase general demand.

The fault lies not in desiring full employment of labor and capital, but rather in failing to see that full employment must result from a combination of two quite different categories of demand: one category is a generalized increase in demand for goods and services; the other is an increase in demand for particular goods and services in particular areas designed to overcome specific problems of unemployment. If governments give the top priority to measures to increase general demand, the special problems are likely to remain unsolved.

Analysis can reveal at what levels of average unemployment countries are likely to experience symptoms of inflation. Hard-core unemployment or its equivalent can be identified. We currently tend to accept historical experience as inevitably indicating the future: to achieve a 4 percent unemployment rate in the United States is to accept, say, 5 percent of price inflation per annum. This is not sensible. First, it misstates the goal which should be to establish a minimum "acceptable" rate of unemployment, that reflects frictional and seasonal unemployment, with no inflation at all. Second, that standard is incomplete. It focuses solely on the average unemployment rate; our attention is not drawn, as it should be, to the composition of that average, and to the problems of hard-core unemployment. Further, with persistent inflation, these relationships constantly change. It means accepting higher rates of inflation to achieve the same average unemployment targets.

The needs are quite clear: we need to revise our concept of "full employment" which is compatible with price stability. Measurements of acceptable unemployment must move away from averages toward ones that indicate the composition of that unemployment. We need to distinguish the level of "average" unemployment compatible with price stability from the unemployment that remains and requires special measures directly targeted at it. Special measures, however, should be most carefully chosen and implemented to suit the problems. Approached this way, full employment and price stability can be compatible.

With new concepts and properly stated goals, we can revise the "game plan": what has to change and how to accomplish such changes? Are such changes "feasible"? If not, why not? Is it because of certain rigid, hard facts of life or because of political concerns about public reaction? What are those "facts" and "concerns"? Are they, in fact, as unchangeable as we assume? Or, given clear statements of the alternatives, would there be greater flexibility in reaction? The public needs to understand what choices they are really making and what the real options are.

Clearly much of the difficulty of dealing with persistent inflation is that the preventive measures have not been taken soon enough. But inflation has to be dealt with as a fact. There is no choice but to start with the inherited past.

Controls on Prices and Wages

The introduction of comprehensive governmental controls to keep down prices and wages confirms the presence and power of inflationary pressures. In most cases, controls exist because the government has despaired of other ways of attaining equilibrium between supply and demand, that is, of keeping down prices and wages without direct government intervention in the price-market system.

Controls over prices and wages need, however, to be distinguished from various other kinds of governmental measures which increase government's control over economic behavior. Some of these instruments are time-honored: coining and printing of money, monetary policy, taxation, tariffs, subsidies to farmers, public investment in roads. Some are newer: large-scale welfare payments, educational allowances, subsidized food consumption, large-scale support of research, foreign exchange controls. In all these cases and more, the government has some control, but it still relies most heavily on the market-price mechanism with its direct impact on consumption and investment to determine the level and pattern of prices and wages. This is far removed from centralized control of the whole economy as practiced in the Soviet Union and similar economies: it does not include government or community ownership of most industry, agriculture, and trading; production and consumption are not directed from the top.

As with so many other economic and social policies, it is too easily assumed that what might appear to have worked in another economy, or in the same economy under different conditions, can be successfully imitated. In the United

States, the resort to controls clearly reflected deep anxieties about the ability to reduce sufficiently a high rate of inflation (5 percent per annum and more) without bringing about a major recession in business activity and therefore in incomes and employment. The U.S. government faced a dilemma. It perceived the domestic and international ill effects of inflation. But the price to pay for ending the inflation by traditional methods — or even for reducing it to "acceptable" levels — seemed impossibly high. Yet the persistence of inflation and of inflationary expectations had gathered momentum; ultimately they became too strong. Trade unions negotiated wage contracts for one, two, or three years, for wage increases of unprecedented magnitudes anticipating expected future price rises, instead of merely compensating for past price rises plus expected increases in productivity. Most nonunionized employees obtained, or expected to obtain, similar treatment. Firms planned to pass on the increased costs to the purchasers of their commodities. The constituency for keeping down prices became smaller; many were confident of being able to obtain higher money incomes, thereby maintaining their living standards despite rising prices. Others, who could not expect their income to rise as rapidly as the inflation, were grievously hurt. They were numerically large but had little political clout, while those who believed that they could protect themselves were politically powerful. The fact that persistent inflation was strong and injuring most people as in most other countries did not seem to be seen despite signs of increasing unease.

The apparent choice was between more unemployment and more price rises. Unemployment was, understandably, regarded as the greater evil. Most people, even in the very groups which were not able to cope with inflation, seemed to favor accepting inflation — perhaps on the sound but superficial reasoning that some income, regardless of its nominal nature, is better than none. The government did not feel able to act to end price rises; instead, it chose the target of reducing the rate of inflation. Thus, it did not act to end inflationary expectations, and in consequence placed the whole program in jeopardy from its very beginning. The U.S. government seemed unable or unwilling to consider a fundamental attack on the causes of persistent inflation. It dramatically joined the other countries that had failed to find a successful answer to the problem of persistent inflation. It introduced controls designed to put a lid on the boiling pot. It hoped that by so doing the water would cool, the inflationary pressures be reduced and eventually eliminated. It did not appear to see how much fuel remained to keep the water boiling. Controls mean passing from a phase of open inflation to one of suppressed inflation, one that might temporarily be more comfortable and tolerable. But the phase can only be temporary and the price-wage controls will fail unless the intervening period is used to dampen the flames sufficiently by dealing with the underlying causes of persistent inflation.

14

Economic Distortions

Irrationality of Consumption

People decide what they want to do with their money. People shop; they choose, they buy, they pay. These are deliberate actions. Prices guide these decisions. People are price "sensitive"; it matters to them whether things cost more or less, just as it matters whether they have the money (or credit) with which to pay. Price signals, particularly trends in prices and changes in relative prices, make possible the incalculable number of daily economic decisions — made with a minimum of disorder and even with some satisfaction and pleasure.

Despite the multitude and variety of people, firms, and transactions, the underlying rational basis has provided a high degree of predictability to the entire process. When the process becomes irrational and unpredictable, it breaks down. Persistent inflation makes it irrational and unpredictable. In continuing inflation, individuals still go through the motions of economic activities. They sell, buy, exchange; they seek the greatest possible satisfaction from expenditures; they seek to maximize their income. But persistent inflation changes and keeps changing the environment and the market signals. Rational economic decision becomes increasingly difficult, and eventually economic decision-making becomes virtually irrational.

The environment facing the modern consumer is partially illustrated by what is happening in retail distribution. The package with the printed price is disappearing. Not that long ago, the printed price used to be useful, largely as a sales gimmick. The retailer was frequently prepared to sell at below the printed or "listed" price; his actual selling price seemed to be a bargain. At some point in the inflationary process, the printed price became the actual price. More recently in some countries, the printed prices on packages have been stamped over, raising the actual price. A succession of other devices sought less embarrassing ways to indicate new prices. The most recent (though not necessarily the final) one has been to eliminate the printed price from the package; prices can then be shown in some manner which allows for frequent raises.

Irrational consumer behavior is not new; what is new is how large a part it plays in economic and social life and how widespread the behavior has become. The "conspicuous consumption" of the few in previous periods becomes the frenetic behavior of many. Despite unprecedented increases in output and income per person, inflation has distorted consumption patterns, resulting in hardships for a great many and only ephemeral satisfactions and often frustration for others. The distortions are themselves fostered by "consumerism" running rampant in inflation.

Consumer goods are usually categorized as "durables" and

"nondurables." Consumerism has spurred the trend to regard all goods as nondurable. Modern society is becoming a "junk" society: nothing is durable. Repair gives way to replacement of parts — or indeed products — as labor becomes expensive. Then replacement of parts gives way to quick replacement of entire products because the "old" parts are no longer available for the "new" model. New is assumed "better," even if less durable than the old. "Keeping up with the Joneses" requires slavish following of ever-changing fads and models: just having two automobiles, as your neighbors do, is not enough; they must be equally new, and equally expensive. Television sets, washing machines, ski boots, and automobiles — even houses — either do not last or go "out of fashion," and need, accordingly, to be discarded. Durability only means that the product will be outdated by a "new model" before it is worn out; perhaps the vestige of a puritanical instinct occasionally prevents the modern consumer from buying a new product and discarding for "frivolous" reasons — like fashion — the product which he owns and which still functions properly and on which, perhaps, he has not even completed payments. Frequently a "new" model merely looks somewhat different; it may have a minor technical modification rather than a major technological improvement. Advertising and credit facilities together with constant technological improvements lure the purchaser, reminding him repeatedly that, however high the price may seem, it will be even higher, more costly, in the future.

In many countries, families own television sets even at the expense of adequate diet or clothing. Perhaps this is right.

Social psychologists may explain that the very inadequacies of basic necessities heighten the need for some form of entertainment like television. Surely, it should be a matter of personal choice. But it is one thing when the decision to purchase one good or service as against another is the consequence of thoughtfully felt needs and tastes. It is quite another matter when the purchase is artificially stimulated by concern about shifts in future prices, or is induced by high-pressure salesmanship. Commodities are sold for utilities and qualities they do not possess; credit facilities, at hidden high costs, make it all possible. It is also different when government policies aid and encourage this wasteful pattern of consumption. In many countries, consumer credit is more easily obtained for a new television set than for food or housing or even clothing. With a large part of income committed to installments on consumer-durables, too little may remain for other purchases. The consumer is trapped. He is rational after the fact, not before. He may suffer from senseless buying hangovers as he would from alcoholic hangovers. "Caveat emptor" — let the buyer beware — takes on cynical and sinister proportions. Persistent inflation has helped build prosperity on credit-induced consumption. But to stop credit is to risk unemployment and recession.

It is normal to think that consumers satisfy their "needs," then their "wants," and, lastly, their "dreams." Consumerism, fostered by inflation, distorts the emphasis in consumption: highly priced, luxuries take on excessive significance. Luxuries are most likely to be sold more profitably in an inflationary environment. Examples abound everywhere — luxury apartments, large automobiles, expensive clothing and jewels, lavish tours and hotels, "three-star" restaurants, costly country clubs. It is not simply that the same things have become more expensive: an ice cream cone is essentially the same thing whether it costs 5 cents or 25 cents. Instead, the products consumed differ. Ice cream cones are replaced by much more expensive sweets. The bicycle for children is replaced by the small motorbike; the snowmobile is used for winter hunting instead of snowshoes or skis.

Again, credit availability for specific purchases may provide part of the explanation for the shift in consumption. Lending money becomes a new kind of business, characterized by "imagination," "vigor," "initiative," instead of "caution," "austerity," and "passivity." The cold, glassy eye of the banker is replaced by the warm, welcoming handshake. Thus, countries with persistent inflationary conditions have seen the rapid expansion of new financing institutions, selling credit with techniques of high-pressure salesmanship. Banks often find themselves constrained by legal limitations and customs and conventions, while new nonbank (but still lending) institutions finance consumption, often in an unconscionable manner. The costs to the borrowers can be very high and often hidden. But cost should not be measured only in money: living is made even less secure and more miserable by these "financial facilities."

During persistent inflation, "everybody floats, nobody drowns" seems to be the prevalent psychology among many groups in many countries. It means new attitudes toward future income, employment, prices, and wages. Future increases in all are widely accepted as inevitable. The willingness to increase indebtedness, even during periods of increasing unemployment, goes far toward explaining the continuation of consumer booms during recessions.

Consumer-credit figures are available for some countries for a sufficiently long period of time to observe trends. They show very large increases in consumer credit in one country after another. The American style of "buy now, pay later" has overcome cultural patterns that once regarded large-scale installment or hire-purchase buying as signs of personal irresponsibility and poor household financial management. Now it prevails virtually everywhere. Ironically, consumer credit itself could play a most constructive role in society. On reasonable terms and in magnitudes related to capacity to pay, it can facilitate the enjoyment of a higher living standard and even induce higher savings in the form of repayment of debt. It becomes dangerous when it becomes a vehicle of encouraging consumption with little concern for total economic and social costs, paving the way for the "junk" society of today. It is dangerous when it induces low-income groups to buy products at fantastically high rates of interest or, too often, have to default on payments and see their purchases repossessed, for example, cars in the United States. When these sorts of things happen, the credit mechanism can undermine the attempt to achieve sustained improved ways of life, with particularly severe repercussions on the lowest income groups.

But the ability, particularly in inflation, to go into debt is further buttressed by a willingness to do so. That willingness flourishes in an environment of consumerism, itself nourished by reasoning that seeks real assets in a time of persistent inflation and by the prevailing optimism about future increases in income (or debt).

Of course, this is *not* to argue that all, or even most, consumption in an inflationary environment is wrong or bad. Most consumption still consists of needs and reasonable wants. Even luxurious consumption may be desirable in giving a culture its "tone" and "style" — encouraging new art and new music. Even interest in antiques and Oriental rugs as hedges against inflation has by-products in cultural gains such as more widespread appreciation and use of beautiful things. However, whatever its beneficial effects, it is the motivation that is perverted. Inflation induces not the creation or possession of beauty, but the creation or possession of a hedge against inflation. Like everything else it touches, it can distort such creative activity and tastes for its products.

Changed Forms of Savings

An inflationary environment induces a basic change in the behavior of individuals and firms. To generalize, everyone tends quite consciously to "invest" rather than save. No longer does the conscious investor represent a small (very small, in the cases of most developing countries) proportion of the population. The saver, investor, and speculator tend to be combined in the same person.

Farmers have always invested. They set aside seeds, build irrigation ditches and dikes, buy implements. But under inflationary conditions many farmers speculate in land; they hold farms for hoped-for gain in their money values. Or, in France and India, for example, farmers increase their gold holdings over and above those held for traditional purposes like wedding dowries, or burials, because they believe gold to be the only medium of exchange that will assuredly maintain its purchasing power in an inflationary world. Or, if the farmers can raise the capital to do so and their holdings are sufficiently large, they adopt more capital-intensive farming methods. They do so primarily because they judge that during persistent inflation wages and other costs of production are likely to rise relatively rapidly. This increases the already intractable problem of very large unemployment in the developing countries as the displaced farm people go in vain to the cities to find alternative employment.

Urban dwellers, by contrast, normally do very little in these rather habitual forms of investment. The change in their behavior with inflation is, however, often more dramatic than that of the farmer. The urban dweller also seeks "investment" opportunities. Most, however, seek first to protect the purchasing power of their income from inflation's deleterious effects. Some are forced to "moonlight," to take on additional jobs in order to supplement primary incomes no longer adequate to cover the costs of daily needs. Teachers who drive taxis or sell in stores on weekends are familiar in the American scene. Others can, and do, base their selection of jobs — or indeed careers — in no small part on which better protects the value of earnings from inflation. Firms in the United States — whether as a result of competition for employees, or of pressures from labor unions or from the public sector — have had to devise means of meeting these concerns and needs. Cost-of-living clauses in labor contracts, stock options, and profit-sharing schemes are but a few examples of the type of benefits offered.

Particularly those whose incomes have risen — even temporarily — faster than the cost of living can afford to speculate: they search for opportunities to buy assets whose nominal value will rise with, or more than, the general price level. Many invest available funds where the return is highest — even if the venture is quite risky. Others remain satisfied by the prospect of a somewhat lesser but more certain return. Need, and at times the thrill of the game of speculation combine with rising money incomes to nurture the growth of "investors" and "investment."

Competition for the individual's funds, by firms and insurance companies, by trust and pension funds, becomes very intense. Those competing for such funds design assets to meet investors' requirements: new stock issues abound; mutual funds are formed which grow at astronomical rates; when the public grows tired of mutual funds, new forms of assets appear. Bonds issued in some countries provide for automatic adjustment in their capital values to compensate for an erosion in purchasing power. This has been done in various ways: capital values are adjusted according to changes in a specified price index, or the bond value is guaranteed in terms of a foreign currency. Investment in growth stocks and in mutual funds by small investors in the United States and, more recently, in Europe has been an outstanding example of this trend. This differs from savings in a banking system which can then be "mobilized" by the investors who borrow from the banks. It differs from the purchase of bonds of government entities or private corporations which provide the security of a low-risk fixed-income asset.

Fortunately, disincentives to save or incentives to change

the form of saving in an inflationary environment have been partly offset by institutional changes. These have encouraged savings by making them automatic or so disguised that they no longer have the character of "voluntary" savings. Often, these take the form of insurance — life, accident, automobile, fire and theft. But more and more, antiques, paintings, Persian rugs, as well as real estate and equities compete with life insurance as ways of providing an estate for heirs protected against persistent inflation. Similarly, pension funds accumulate; but everywhere growing dissatisfaction with traditional pensions has forced these funds, like some insurance policies, to provide for automatic increases with the cost of living.

Persistent inflation also discourages personal savings. The "money illusion" and improved institutional facilities may sustain personal saving in some countries for some years — even after it has ceased to make economic sense. But, like purchasing power, the habit of saving can and does erode. If inflation persists, the only unpredictable thing is when the erosion will become noticeable. That this will happen is virtually certain.

Persistent inflation has augmented the gap between needed and actual savings. Savings are, in consequence, chronically inadequate. The records of the United States and Britain have been among the poorest in this respect. The pull of consumption undoubtedly has been a major factor in explaining this savings performance, but the outlook for price rises has also been important. Since the continuation of inflationary conditions has, over the years, discouraged savings of the more traditional type, some national governments have had to cease borrowing from their citizens during inflationary periods; they turn to their printing presses to provide needed money. This, of course, further aggravates the inflationary pressures and their effects.

Investment Uncertainties

Major distortions in investments reflect the distortions in consumption; however irrationally the demand may be created, economies produce and distribute what is demanded.

Firms can cope with some of the internal mechanics of inflation: the need to revalue assets — plants, equipment, and inventories; the need to change ways of raising funds; the need to revamp pension funds to provide for increases in cost of living. But the changes in business practices caused by persistent inflation are unfortunately both more profound and more disturbing than these. They are grounded in the uncertainties and risks created by persistent inflation. These alter the investment climate and, therefore, have a major impact on production.

The difficulties in business planning under persistent inflation stem, in no small part, from the uncertainties as to the future course of prices. Persistent inflation creates a whole series of unpredictable changes resulting from factors baffling to the individual consumer or firm. The direction of change of the average level of prices may be predictably upward, but the rate of change is not likely to be predictable. Further, the effect of inflation on relative prices no longer makes it possible for even the more sophisticated businessman to feel that he has a grasp on his own costs and final prices, much less those of his competitors or those in possible alternative activities in which he might invest.

The banking system is undergoing a parallel experience. Commercial banks which used to regard their business as short-term lending to business firms to finance holdings of inventories have gone in for long-term loans and mortgage commitments which combine higher earnings with marketability. Demand-deposit liabilities are balanced increasingly by long-term, less liquid assets.

A businessman watching these developments cannot but wonder how long the process can continue. Will he suddenly find that all-important credit in increasing amounts is no longer available? Is it a bubble that will burst — comparable to 1929? He cannot act on this assumption, but his confidence in the future becomes a curious mixture of certainty in continuing price rises and credit availability, coupled with growing anxieties.

15

Handicaps
to Economic Management

The distortion of consumption and investment, and the changed forms of savings handicap growth and development in both developed and less developed countries. It may be argued that with large underemployed resources, in the form of capital or labor, increased prices will act as an incentive to increase output, hopefully increasing employment and, at some point, increasing investment. In countries like Japan and Brazil, continuing price rises have probably helped to increase output and output capacity. There, wages and incomes were held lower in some productive areas than others, inducing labor and capital to move into more productive sectors. By careful governmental and business policies, the impact of inflation benefited some and hurt others in order to increase the national capacity to produce. This process can go on in some countries for a period of years. However, as the inflation persists, bottlenecks appear: certain critical skills become scarce, even when the average level of unemployment is still rather high; wage increases precede price increases and are generalized over the entire economy, including firms and industries with very low productivity gains; credit becomes too expensive; public services become inadequate. In addition, domestic markets remain too small while international competition requires that wage and other costs be in line with international developments. These bottlenecks make it increasingly difficult to achieve full employment without accelerating inflation.

As prices continue to rise and the basic causes of persistent inflation are not overcome, the level of unemployment "compatible" with a certain rate of price increase also rises. It may take, say, 5 percent unemployment to avoid further price rises, whereas previous to the persistent inflation, this may have been achieved at, say 2 percent unemployment. Measures to reduce unemployment may also result in higher rates of price increases. The process of maintaining "full employment" is more bedeviled by inflation than ever before, while the harmful consequences of the continuing inflation make doing something about it more urgent.

The current experiences of high rates of inflation and relatively high rates of unemployment in the United Kingdom and the United States (inflation in the latter temporarily partly repressed by price and wage controls) are only the logical consequences of persistent inflation. The situation will get worse until it is recognized that for full-employment policies to be successfully achieved and maintained, the end of inflationary expectations is required.

Of course, the phenomenal postwar growth has been primarily due to the ability to increase the productivity of labor, combined in many countries with an increase in the labor force. The existence of bottlenecks in the form of labor shortages for certain purposes (and places), together with shortages of capital and changes in management and entrepreneurial attitudes, threaten the continuation of the growth process. In addition to these more traditional bottlenecks there are newer factors like raw-material shortages, environmental pollution, and social disorders. All of the bottlenecks both heighten inflationary pressures and increase in number and intractability in response to the persistent inflation. Thus, we may expect continuing price rises repeatedly to frustrate policies designed to achieve and maintain high levels of employment or economic growth and development until tolerance of continuing price rises comes to an end.

V

A Closer Look at the World
of Persistent Inflation:
Social and Political Effects

16

Why Social and Political?

The twentieth century has been the Century of Inflation. It has also been the era in which more people, in absolute numbers and in relative terms, than ever before, have climbed out of the ditch of animal-like, subsistence standards of living to attain human levels. Two-thirds of the world has, admittedly, yet to attain that human level, but this represents a great improvement since 90 percent or more used to be in the substandard group. It is tempting to see the simultaneous prevalence of inflation with the progress made in reducing poverty either as a positive factor in the progress, or a minor cost: no one wants to jeopardize this progress. Quite the contrary, the need is to accelerate the rate of progress. The economic costs of inflation would be tolerable, some might argue, if its social and political consequences were demonstrably desirable. However, no nation or society, irrespective of what kind it is, can regard the long-run social consequences of persistent inflation as desirable. For the price of persistent inflation is the undermining of any and every form of society and the placing of all future social as well as economic progress in serious jeopardy.

A number of the social and political effects of inflation are readily observable in the experiences of countries throughout the world. Others are less easily traced, but are believed to be largely the result of the environment of persistent inflation. Their full implications require thorough investigation by experts in many different fields of knowledge. In essence, the social and political consequences of inflation result from its uneven effects on different groups within the community. This combines with the very great difficulties that private and governmental institutions have in responding to these consequences, particularly when the very institutions are weakened by inflation. It is only by recognizing its multi-faceted nature that we can hope to cope with it successfully.

Income Inequalities and Social Strains

The inequitable effects on personal incomes provide the backdrop against which the additional social strains caused by persistent inflation can be seen. For many the change in consumption induced by persistent inflation results more from necessity or expectations about future price rises or increases in income and borrowing than from changes in taste. A sharp rise in the cost of services, such as house maintenance, frequently causes the housewife to buy less expensive foods and less desirable clothing to compensate for the unexpectedly large part of family income needed for house maintenance. This situation may even require that she go out to work, though she might prefer to stay home and look after her husband and children.

People with low incomes are in the worst position of all. They may be misspending their meager funds: judged by their own definitions of their needs and wants, fewer of the preferred, less expensive, more durable products are produced; such products disappear from the stores, replaced by more expensive and less durable substitutes. In addition, the "demonstration" effects of luxury consumption make poorer people ever more vividly aware of what they are not attaining and hence they may be chronically dissatisfied.

Moreover, in most modern societies, which have rejected the notion of the inevitability of poverty, the poor have been led to "expect" more. But even significant progress in bettering material conditions and achieving a more satisfactory way of life seems doomed to frustration in the face of widespread and continuing inflationary consumption. As costs increase, activities or products once within the poor man's reach are now quite beyond his grasp. Nothing has replaced the five-cent beer and free snacks on the counter, or the bleacher seats in the ball park. The local cinema is now expensive and the bowling alley increasingly beyond reach. Even within his own city, transportation absorbs an increasing share of income. He may be forced to change his travel habits or even his job to lessen his local travel; it is too expensive to accept employment in other parts of the city, and far too expensive to seek employment elsewhere.

Alienation and Unrest

The much noted anxiety and "alienation" which psychologists and philosophers have pointed to as the consequence of industrialization may well be magnified by this inflationary environment. It simultaneously encourages both a certain life style and a fear that that life style may prove unsustainable. These uncertainties beset modern man because he is too knowledgeable not to realize that science and technology provide the basis for material improvement, but too intelligent to believe the present trends in consumption patterns can go on indefinitely.

In widespread depression, the employed often shared their income with less fortunate members of their family or friends, as well as contributing to charities. During persistent inflation, such humane feelings erode. The young newly-wed couple finds it most difficult to be able to buy the things needed to set up a home. Some decide not to do so and choose "communal" living, sharing their economic and financial burdens by forgoing precious privacy and full use of personal possessions. Others are assisted by parents fortunate enough to be holding their own against inflation. (Some parents are able to do so but are unwilling because they are caught up in their own consumerism.) Parents find that their original expectations of when their children would become self-reliant are not fulfilled. "Children" need continued help well beyond the traditional age of maturity. Assistance is required not only to finish school but to weather low-income periods until their earnings enable young people to cope with inflation, a stage many never seem to reach.

The same erosion happens toward the end of the life span. Savings thought to be adequate prove most inadequate. The high costs of medical care and nursing homes have been well publicized; but the problem extends into all aspects of consumption by "senior citizens" — clothing, vacations, gifts, transportation, newspapers and books, and entertainment. Unexpectedly and unavoidably, people who never thought of themselves as needing financial help — or even expected to help others — find themselves in need and forced to seek their children's or community's help.

At the same time, their children are experiencing the additional pressures of inflation. The need to take care of their elders often materializes as unexpectedly for the young as for the old. The children may even have expected help from their parents. The pressures of persistent inflation clash with the willingness to help, often resulting in feelings of guilt and resentment. The family often proves incapable of providing the protective environment parents would hope to give and children hope to find. Family tensions multiply in societies which are already torn by tensions. And the community's private activities, like charities, churches, and foundations, are undermined by rising costs at the same time that their needs are greatly increased.

Such social ills are generally manifest in unrest on a large scale, in the form of city-wide, regional, or national disturbances; social malaise is also expressed in strains on family relations. At the same time, demands on public services dramatically increase, further contributing to the straining of the social fabric as people challenge the ability and willingness of government mechanisms and officials adequately to cope with their problems.

Inflation alone cannot, of course, be blamed for all the many malaises which trouble societies everywhere — the increase in crimes, prevalence of social violence, the greater use of drugs, the disregard for individuals, the widening sense of alienation and drift, the cynicism of many toward government and toward the "naïve" belief in the desirability of devotion to public duty, the increasing skepticism in the possibility or even desirability of human progress, and so forth. The persistence of inflation and the government's repeated failures, despite promises to the contrary, to eliminate it have weakened society's ability to cope successfully with such malaise as well as increased skepticism about the intentions or ability of government to provide the answers to current social and economic difficulties.

Some may argue that the answer lies in less government — we already have too much of it. Weaker governments are less likely to lead us to Orwell's *1984!* Perhaps so. But, paradoxically, persistent inflation, which is both caused by inadequate government and results in heightened disbelief in government, has resulted in increased reliance upon it. Indeed, more and more people turn to it as the "only" way out.

17

Repercussions
for Political Systems

Persistent inflation also has profound implications for political systems. Because of social difficulties it fosters, as well as its harmful income-distribution effects, inflation creates grave problems for modern governments while at the same time it weakens their capacity to solve these problems. Indeed, in virtually all cases of major political upheaval in the postwar period, inflation has been a common element of such upheavals. The direct reasons are found essentially in the impact which the persistent inflation has on the attitudes and behavior of those at all levels of public service whose activities provide the governmental framework within which all private activities take place. Inflation also introduces other weaknesses in political systems. Governments have to end inflationary trends while coping with conditions created by past inflations. Inequalities and distortions inherited from the past thwart and frequently paralyze governments into inaction.

Vulnerability of Modern Societies

The size, complexities, and weblike interrelations of activities of modern economies and societies result in many "critical" points. At these critical points social and economic life can be disrupted by the malfunctioning of public systems, such as electric power and water supply, garbage collection, transportation, policing, and teaching. At these same critical points there are people, not just machines. Without the effective performance of these people, societies can be brought to a standstill. Yet it is these people who are very often hard hit by inflation and whose strategic importance must be recognized when governments try to end persistent inflation. Even the threat of a strike can be most disturbing. Now, in addition to traditional strikes, labor has adopted other techniques — sit-ins and slow-downs. These have become fashionable and, like all fashions, have quickly spread around the world. Argentina, France, the United Kingdom, and others have all undergone such experiences. This vulnerability is new and the power of those who work the levers of organized society at the critical points, already augmented, will continue to increase as the conditions of modern societies enhance it.

Persistent inflation thus exacerbates relations between labor and government, perhaps even more so than those between labor and private management. Labor disputes now occur quite commonly in occupations in which they had previously been rare events — protests are heard from police, customs officials, teachers, sanitation workers, prison guards, public utilities. The unconscious assumption that all sorts of activities, disputes, and changes can take place within a society, and that "someone" will still take care of the essentials is no longer valid.

Inflation has made "workers" and "trade unionists" out of

public officials and members of professional societies. Headlines in all countries tell of policemen, garbage collectors, teachers, communication and transport workers on strike. This testifies dramatically to the role of persistent inflation in making such people feel cheated and deprived; they lose their sense of public service as they find themselves, year after year, unable to cope successfully with the effects of inflation, despite assured money income. For many, the foremost problem is not lowered standards of living — but rather maintenance of what they have come to regard as deserved living standards. Ironically, this change in the character and attitude of public servants and the decline in the public regard for government have come at the very stage in history when government has assumed the leading role in society.

Tax Revolt and Expenditures Ambivalence

Surveys indicate that despite the increased expenditures for public services in the United States, as elsewhere, taxpayers and homeowners complain constantly that they pay more for services that are at best no better than five years ago, and often worse. Taxpayers have also become much more sensitive about who benefits from these expenditures — an element of increasing selfishness that does not augur well for the future. If it continues, it will represent a fundamental change in public philosophy. The United States has prided itself on its mobility based, in part, on providing the means to poorer groups to improve their status by taxing the more affluent; taxation has been based on ability to pay. Present attitudes, however, seem to associate tax payment closely with benefit received. Childless couples object to school tax payments; state governments object to receiving less in federal benefits than the amounts of tax payments of their citizens. These circumstances greatly weaken the tax mechanism as a tool to achieve social mobility and equity.

In the more populous regions of the United States, between mid-1965 and mid-1970, public welfare costs rose 184 percent, health and hospital expenses 96 percent, police protection 77 percent, and sanitation costs 39 percent. The result has been, of course, a large increase in the need for tax revenues. The desperate search for new tax revenues is reflected in the variety of taxes being introduced or increased. In 1971, 30 out of 50 states raised their tax rates in some form or other, as did most of the nation's larger municipalities. Fifteen of the 30 states raised personal and corporate income taxes, and five others adopted new forms of these taxes. Five states increased their sales tax rates. Eighteen increased tobacco taxes, while eight increased taxes on consumption of alcohol. Sixteen others tapped motorists by either raising gasoline taxes or vehicle-use taxes or both.

The citizen sees himself pounded by two stones — the one, the reduction in the purchasing power of his income; the other, the decrease in after-tax income as experts figure out new ways to obtain revenues for government. The taxpayer becomes an angry citizen open to emotional appeals for irrational behavior. Instead of directing his wrath against the harmful and unnecessary inflation, he often attacks the taxes which are needed to pay for the very public services which he strenuously advocates. Thus, in the United States the specter of tax revolt looms. These sentiments are world-wide.

Tax revolt is the logical consequence of continuing inflation, not only because taxes are high, but also because of an increasing lack of sympathy for the purposes for which revenues are spent and an increasing lack of confidence in the governments collecting and spending them. People complain that taxes are rising and becoming too high. More fundamentally, they complain about the new pattern of income distribution and consumption resulting from the way in which tax revenues are spent.

High levels of government expenditures are frequently criticized. Some are critical because of the purposes for which the monies are spent; others because of the resulting tax burdens; some because of the inflationary consequences. Among the last group, criticism is particularly sharp if the expenditures are financed in considerable measure by borrowing from the banking system or by direct use of the government printing press. (Both means expand the money supply to finance the larger government expenditures rather than increase tax revenues or tap voluntary savings.)

Whatever their political ideologies, the finance minister (or secretary of the treasury), often in alliance with the head of the central bank, usually leads the crusade to keep down government expenditure. These monetary and financial officials are those who must find funds to finance expenditures; as such, they find themselves in repeated confrontation with other government departments. The head of the central bank must be concerned about the internal price effects and external (balance-of-payments) effects of government expenditures, particularly — as often happens — where any resultant budget deficits must be financed by increases in money and credit. With these responsibilities, he inevitably advocates relatively cautious and conservative budget policies. So do ministers of finance, unless they get politically ambitious!

The line-up, however, is lopsided. Other agencies have constituencies which look to them to spend more, not less; and the public applauds the general prosperity, or the special group improvement. Agricultural workers, children, ill people, veterans, old people, minority groups, students, civil servants, and those with government contracts — road-construction companies, builders, aircraft and munition firms, teachers — all find support for expenditures on their behalf. Firms, trade unions, family relations, community leaders, politicians, publicists, and so forth all can be relied upon to champion their cause. In the end, while budget balancing may be popular as a political slogan, in practice it is the needs of any special group that are considered paramount and virtually irreducible. Consequently, the direction of change in government expenditures is generally upward. The only questions are: How much? How fast? How steadily?

On the other hand, it might be expected that a large and determined constituency would support a reduction in expenditures. In a way there is such a constituency. In a more important way, there is not. Many people, very many, do not like inflation; they suffer from it. But as a political constituency, these people tend to be more potential than actual. That potential is fatally flawed in that the persons and firms who make up this constituency want to make exceptions for those governmental expenditures which are important to them. Otherwise, they of course favor reducing expenditures.

Hence, the easiest way to "cut" government expenditures is to announce that "future" increases will be reduced. Demands for reduction in governmental personnel — at times made in complete ignorance of or disregard for needs, at times made quite intelligently — are met by governments agreeing to reduce these numbers by "attrition," a commitment in the future not to fill vacancies caused by retirement and deaths. Seemingly this hurts no one and is, therefore, politically feasible. These approaches, frequently — even usually — yield nothing, either economically or socially. New government responsibilities continuously arise; promised economies become transparently infeasible. Even attrition is difficult to implement because it means no new positions for eager job seekers and political leaders eager to get their support.

The recourse to the rhetoric of promises does, however, have the virtue of saving face for political leaders, aware of the repercussions of inflation and high taxes but unable for political reasons to act. Where government is held responsible for providing employment, even relatively small-scale unemployment attributable to government actions becomes political dynamite. When, occasionally, effective action to reduce government expenditures is taken — increased bus fares in Mexico, partial elimination of redundant labor in the Argentine state railways, reduced rice subsidies in Ceylon, cutbacks in certain defense contracts in some American cities — the political fallout is very great, even if other governmental expenditures continue to rise. The fact of unemployment in the affected enterprises is not offset by the fact of work for others elsewhere. Similarly, once having accepted responsibility for a level of food consumption, it is most difficult to withdraw from this commitment. On some grounds it may seem obviously logical to do so, but not to those who rely on the government assistance; for them, increased self-reliance means sudden, often severe hardship. Free lunches for children in the public school system in the United States comes to mind as an action designed to meet a widespread social need; once started, it gathered a logic of its own — not the logic of budgets or national economic management. Protecting the existing levels of income, employment, and consumption, whether viewed in general terms or as the problems of particular groups and geographic areas, is now seen to require the corresponding public expenditures despite the inflationary pressures which they generate.

Stabilization Attempts

From time to time, governments adopt "anti-inflationary" policies. In doing so, they are convinced that the repercussions, for the country and its people, of the inflation leave no other option.

At the outset, "anti-inflation" (or "stabilization") measures may have popular support; the public has suffered from continuing inflation and welcomes the prospect of a reduction in the pressures. Workers see that their wages might now be better protected from the erosion. Industrialists see possible opportunities for profit-making in less risky and more enduring productive activities if the stabilization program succeeds. Farmers hope that the price of manufactures will stop rising as rapidly. Government officials and other employees get new hope that the price for holding their more secure jobs is not a sharp decline in real income. Those without incomes are obviously most hopeful. Political leaders and government administrators see the possibility of ending the harmful domestic and external effects. Under a successful stabilization program, budget deficits would decline as tax revenues, still based on inflationary incomes, were maintained, or even rose, relative to expenditures. The balance of payments of the country would markedly improve. This would not only reduce the country's need to depend on foreign financial help, but might even permit relaxation of government controls restraining imports. In a number of cases, the improvement in the balance of payments could enable countries to reduce their external debt and build up monetary reserves to meet future external contingencies. Success would feed on itself, changing attitudes, expectations, and prospects. In the end, the country might also witness a boom in more productive activities, with increased employment and investment.

In many cases, however, such stabilization efforts prove to be only temporary successes; they fail to overcome the obstacles created by persistent inflation. Employees in both the government and private sectors, though hopeful, remain skeptical that the inflation will end; often they have experienced failures of past efforts. They continue to push for higher wages and their case often is very strong. Political leaders find it most difficult to resist such demands. If the budgetary situation improves, political leaders are pressured to use this improvement to increase expenditures. Businessmen, showing the same skepticism of success as others, and loath to be caught in unprofitable activities if the stabilization measures fail, may well adopt a wait-and-see attitude before making new investments. Increased unemployment appears in some areas, and is feared in others. Those in activities profiting from persistent inflation, of course, oppose stabilization. Political opposition to the government usually cannot resist taking advantage of these complaints and the skepticism, even though they know that success of the stabilization would make them more able to govern effectively in the future. In brief, the programs often are given up because too many believe that their interests are served by high government expenditures and freely flowing bank credit, or governments prove incapable of correcting the inequities of the past inflation.

Unless a visible improvement in these inequities can be made and the problems of increased unemployment and business decline can be kept within politically tolerable limits, the anti-inflationary policies fail. Instead of selective wage increases to correct inherited wage distortions, wages in general spurt upward, particularly of those in stronger bargaining positions. High rates of government expenditures then continue and even increase. The effect of the past high levels of expenditures is to perpetuate the apparent need for them, despite their inflationary effects. The rising trend in government expenditures is thus more than a reflection of rising prices and wages; the conviction is strengthened that maintenance of politically acceptable economic conditions requires such a trend.

This scenario of the fate of stabilization programs is, of course, highly summarized and simplified. Each program has had its own special features, turns, twists, and, of course, results. But the basic sequence of the scenario has been often repeated — despair with allowing the continuation of inflation, the presence of political leaders willing to take the known political risks, the initial favorable public reaction and well-received and highly publicized improvements, the failure of the government to recognize the strength of inflationary expectations and the inherited inequities of the past, followed by the inability of the government to persist in its announced and implemented policies, and the quick and strong revival of skepticism giving new life and vigor to inflationary expectations.

The history of stabilization programs underlines the point that, in the public mind, the government makes or breaks national prosperity. And no postwar government, at least none in the Western world, has been able to survive a public view that it is prolonging a recession. As in so many other things, all types of governments have "proved" their superiority in dealing with economic and social affairs — so long as the winds are fair. When an economic gale blows, all kinds of governments face trouble. It is the hard luck of many governments to be in office when inflationary pressures are so great that the application of severe contracting brakes becomes inevitable. The consequences are often a sudden interest in national policies and dissatisfaction with whatever government is in power, irrespective of its political form. One reason why it is politically more possible now to be against inflation is that in many countries it is being accompanied by unacceptable levels of unemployment.

Budget and Time Lags

Persistent inflations thus greatly strengthen the fundamental political difficulties in pursuing fiscal policies designed to avoid, reduce, or eliminate inflationary pressures. These difficulties are enhanced by others. One is the legislative process through which most national budgets must pass.

Generally, legislatures enact budgets, but the degree of executive influence over legislation varies greatly. In some countries, like the United States and the Philippines, legislatures have prided themselves on their separation and independence from the executive. Indeed, in such countries, despite great care in advance preparation in putting together the budget, its enactment into law is frequently very difficult, long-delayed, and done only after considerable significant amendment. Other countries, like the United Kingdom and India, have parliamentary systems dominated by a prime minister and his cabinet, all of whom are members of the legislature. Nevertheless, the cabinet must and does pay close attention to the wishes and needs of the members of the legislature, particularly those in its own party. These members are influenced by pressure groups and special interests, especially in their constituency. This is seen repeatedly when "bread and butter" issues like employment, taxation, welfare measures, and prices are considered. These issues, visibly, directly, and usually quickly affect the constituents of members of the legislature. These constituents decide the fate of their representatives and thereby of the cabinet. Thus, even ministers in parliamentary systems are severely limited in their actual freedom to propose legislation even though, since they are not in a congressional system, what they propose is most likely to be accepted.

Some legislatures — and this is frequent — have no majority party; the leadership is formed by a coalition of parties. Legislative majorities are then hard to achieve and at least feared to be easy to lose. Budgets, moreover, frequently cause the coalition to collapse — and a "safe" budget and an anti-inflationary budget are only rare coincidents. It is easier to "give" something to everyone in a coalition than to "take" something from one or all. Even military governments find their budgetary actions the subject of intense public discussion and political opposition and are sensitive to public reactions to their budgetary policies.

The budget itself poses obstacles to anti-inflationary policies. It is a sluggish instrument of policy. Given the importance of the public sector in many economies, and the difficulties it faces in making important changes in taxation and expenditures, it is not surprising that budgetary actions are hard to keep in tune with a dynamic, changing economic situation. By the time a tax program to encourage investment or consumption is passed, it may well prove too little and far too late. Budgetary actions are frequently like trains going over mountains — round and round on slopes engineered to avoid slipping backward, with much huffing and puffing, and seemingly no way of going faster without risking complete breakdown and wreckage.

Even assuming that budgetary actions are adopted in time — a rare occurrence in most countries — implementation usually takes some time. Changes in corporate or personal income taxes take time to have important effects.

The taxes are usually collected months after the measures have been passed — and even more months or years after they were first introduced. Similarly, certain expenditures like road-building, public housing, bridges, schools, and new armament programs, take years to implement. The time factor makes successful economic management even more difficult.

Certain tax rates can be increased and the increased taxes collected with relative speed; this is true of excise taxes on consumption goods or turnover taxes at various stages of the productive process, among others. These means may, however, be ill-suited to the economy's needs. Further, they may meet political and social opposition; sales taxes that are applied uniformly are "regressive" — they impose relatively greater burdens on lower-income groups. Other expenditures can be rapidly implemented and have quick effects on the economy; increases in pay, welfare payments, and veterans bonuses are examples of this. Conversely, these kinds of taxes and expenditures can be used to contract economies rapidly. But the political difficulties of attaining legislative support to restrain inflation have usually been incomparably greater than in cases of expansive measures.

On balance, though there may be theoretical symmetry between quick-acting and slow-acting budgetary activities, the political attitudes toward these measures are most asymmetrical. A pay increase for government employees can often be passed quickly and can have a quick effect, but a decrease in government salaries is seldom politically feasible, though its effects would also be quick.

These limitations on governmental actions help explain

why budgetary actions tend to be too little or too late in dealing with inflation. This is particularly true when inflation has persisted. Effective action then becomes a political nightmare.

The Credibility Gap

This situation also helps explain another nearly universal phenomenon — the growing lack of credibility of governments. In many countries the public simply does not accept what government officials tell it. This may not be a question of disbelief; rather it is an attitude of profound skepticism. Government after government comes to office — by vote or otherwise — pledged to end inflation, reduce "wasteful" or "excessive" public expenditures, refrain from increasing taxes if not reduce them, restore external financial soundness, increase investment and growth, improve material well-being, particularly for the poorer groups. (Some regard this pattern of promises and slogans as peculiar to their country; actually, the language may differ, but the content is markedly similar from country to country.) Some of these promises are, of course, made with tongue in cheek. But many are not. Many are simply naïve, ignoring the deep roots of modern societal ills; many ignore key political facts — the difficulties of budgetary procedures, the lack of public interest and support for such legislation, the inevitable time lags between legislation and its effects, even if enactment is finally achieved, and the relatively small portion of the budget that any new government can change.

The credibility gap in public economic policy is particularly significant. That is an area where the government says it can act effectively; moreover, the public expects it to perform effectively. Budgets, monetary policy, and public investment decisions are complex matters, fraught with the difficulties of decision-making and implementation; but they fall within the highly advertised competency of government officials and experts. Moreover, they do not seem to require international support.

How does one break the vicious circle of irresponsible promises, induced by a combination of ignorance and eagerness for public support, leading to inevitable failures, leading in turn to public disillusionment and discontent, and this in turn, to more irresponsible promises? The answer is not only of critical importance for eliminating persistent inflation; it affects the very viability of governments in modern societies.

VI

Persistent Inflation
and the International
Monetary System

18

Experience of the United Kingdom and the United States

The existence of persistent inflation leads to repeated balance-of-payments crises and a resultant need for relatively frequent currency devaluations; often the devaluations are even greater in magnitude than the domestic inflation. Currency devaluations, in turn, may strengthen domestic inflation and thereby defeat their very purpose unless they are accompanied by measures to prevent such repercussions.

These interrelations between domestic inflation and balance-of-payments behavior have long been recognized, but received little attention in the United States until the New Economic Policy was announced in August 1971. The experiences of the United Kingdom and the United States are worth reviewing, not only because they illustrate the relation between inflation and the balance of payments, but because these two countries' currencies have been by far the most important in the world's monetary system.

United Kingdom

In the United Kingdom, particularly in the 1960s, the "stop-go" policies of successive governments reflected the recogni-

tion that, at some point, domestic inflationary pressures
created by expansionary policies designed to achieve and
maintain full employment ("go") so weakened the external
economic and financial position of the United Kingdom that
the government (Labour or Conservative) felt the need to
restrain the domestic economy ("stop"). It did so particularly by curbing private consumption, reducing the relative
weight of government expenditures, and constraining private
investment. At times it was also thought temporarily necessary to intensify restrictions on imports and on the outflow
of capital; usually exports were the one favored sector. The
United Kingdom, one of the world's largest importing countries, well appreciated that such restrictive policies hurt
countries abroad — those that exported to it as well as those
that benefited from British capital. But the inflation's persistence left no choice. Britain was forced to defend its external balance.

Most difficult of all during periods of restraint, it was
necessary for the United Kingdom to accept higher levels of
unemployment and lower, if not zero, rates of economic
growth. While other countries — among them France and
Italy — had similar experiences, the United Kingdom received the most attention: its currency, the pound sterling,
was widely used in international trade and finance, even in
transactions not involving the United Kingdom. Many
countries held international monetary reserves in sterling;
these sterling balances, though much smaller than those in
U.S. dollars, still amounted to about $6 billion in the mid-
1960s. The United Kingdom's currency shared with the
United States dollar the distinction of being one of the two
truly international currencies.

For centuries, firms and countries all over the world had gone to London to obtain credits and loans, ranging from overnight accommodations to those with many years' maturity. Only the United States had developed comparably large banking and capital-raising facilities. The "City" of London, as in the past, is a great broker between people all over the world who have funds to lend and those who wish to borrow.

Britain's balance-of-payments crises, however, reduced countries' and individuals' willingness to hold liquid savings or international assets in sterling. It was critically important to be able easily and without loss to exchange sterling assets for other foreign currencies, when and if needed, to make international payments in other currencies, most frequently the U.S. dollar. Yet balance-of-payments crises always bring the threat of governmental controls over the free use of such assets and recurrent crises increase the likelihood of devaluation, resulting in losses to foreigners who hold those assets.

Other countries' practice of holding monetary reserves in sterling did have many advantages for the United Kingdom. With a number of countries, it could finance any deficits in its payments with its own currency — sterling. It meant increasing sterling liabilities to foreigners, but it was virtually equivalent to having automatic international credit facilities. In addition, these sterling balances represented investments of savings in the United Kingdom by foreign individuals, firms, and countries. It was largely through such sterling holdings that Britain mobilized savings from abroad. These, in turn, were used by Britain to lend abroad. This had been a lucrative source of profit for private firms and of foreign exchange for the national economy. A reduction in the willingness to hold sterling assets therefore also reduced the scope of and profit from British lending activities, further deteriorating the balance of payments.

One consequence of this situation was to push the City of London to preserve its role as one of the world's leading financial centers by becoming a center for financial transactions in currencies other than sterling — the celebrated Euro-dollar market — taking advantage of limitations placed by the United States on external financial transactions in U.S. financial markets. Although British firms have profited greatly by extending credit facilities in Euro-currencies, they have also had to pay sufficient interest to attract foreigners to deposit funds in London, narrowing the range of profitability.

The Americans were always among the most staunch supporters of the United Kingdom during repeated balance-of-payments crises. Partly this was for sentimental and political reasons; it was, however, also in recognition of the major role of Britain and sterling in the international economy. The United States repeatedly helped take the lead — by itself and with other countries and in international institutions — in offering assistance to cope with these crises.

But neither the British genius for government, nor their sophistication in economic science, nor the help of the United States and other countries could cope with the basic cause of the repeated crises — the persistent inflation and the resulting inflationary expectations. A formula for achieving acceptably low levels of unemployment (about 2 percent or less) and adequate growth (about 3 to 4 percent per annum) without getting into balance-of-payments crises could not be found. Widespread study of British experience greatly enlightened the economic theorist, stimulating him to more sophisticated analyses of the causes and effects of inflation. Unfortunately, the theories remained oversimplified: they failed to give adequate attention to the underlying causes, effects, and interactions of persistent inflation. Since no British government successfully addressed itself to these aspects, the inflationary trend continued to gather strength.

As long as external conditions were favorable, as long as high levels of demand prevailed abroad and — even better — if inflation in competing industrial countries was stronger than in the United Kingdom, or while the British competitive position still benefited by devaluations of sterling (in 1949 and 1967), the balance-of-payments impact of the persistent inflation, however bad, was obscured. The situation could remain tolerable. But when external conditions turned less favorable, the persistence of domestic inflation re-created the crises; measures to restrain the economy again became necessary. Had it been able to end these repeated crises, the United Kingdom might not have slipped from having the third highest income per capita in the world (after the United States and Canada) to the lower ranks of the industrial nations; it has been overtaken, for example, by Germany, Australia, and Sweden, and is rapidly being gained on by Italy and Japan. The United Kingdom, which had flourished in previous centuries in a world of expanding world trade, had to accept a sharply shrinking proportion of world trade. Ironically, this took place just when the expansion of world trade took on an unprecedented magnitude and persistency. The world's leading trading nation was unable to profit sufficiently from a world environment which otherwise might have been expected to be particularly favorable to it.

Nobody gained from the decline of the relative position of the United Kingdom. Put differently, all — including its competitors — would have benefited from a more success-fully managed and expanding U.K. economy. Despite the efforts of the British financial and monetary authorities throughout the postwar years, and their reluctance to take the seemingly easy way out — the more frequent devalua-tion of sterling that some urged — persistent inflation was not dealt with effectively. This is not to argue that monetary and fiscal policies were not "tough" enough, or that the authorities lacked the wisdom, conviction, and courage to act (though, at times, delays may have been excessive). Perhaps their policy was not effective because the British were too narrowly preoccupied with the external aspects of continu-ing inflation — the balance of payments. In consequence, inadequate public attention was given to the costs, in reducing the relative material and social well-being of the British people, of failure to solve the problem of persistent inflation. The underlying nature of persistent inflation was not suf-ficiently comprehended; it therefore could not have been tackled effectively. Without a successful attack on persistent inflation, no balance-of-payments policy could have been — or indeed can be — successful for any sustained period of time.

United States

In the United States, the situation was quite different. Some monetary and financial officials might worry about the interrelation between inflation and the balance of payments, but the public at large remained blissfully unaware, and political leaders reflected this joyful ignorance. Indeed, many experts were available in the United States to assure everyone that "creeping" inflation was a good thing. When it became clear that the creep had progressed to a crawl, than a walk, and finally a rapid walk, if not a run, and that the external difficulties could no longer be ignored, awareness grew, even if only belatedly and in limited circles.

The New Economic Policy adopted in August 1971 encompassed measures directed at correcting the internal domestic inflation and improving the balance of payments. Nevertheless, the fact that the United States' balance-of-payments difficulties were intimately related to its persistent inflation was barely mentioned. While nodding at a trade-account deficit, explanations of the payments difficulties more frequently emphasized the effects on the capital account of the U.S. recession in 1970 and 1971: the recession had led to lower interest rates and easier credit policies; with interest rates higher and credit tighter in Europe and Japan, many there were eager to borrow from the United States and large amounts of capital flowed out of the country.

When the balance of payments of the United States is analyzed in detail, particularly focusing on those items that are affected by relative international competitiveness, the great influence of the persistent inflation on the balance of payments emerges. Set aside the capital account of the balance of payments — largely foreign lending and investments — and take the trade accounts: exports and imports. For many years, the U.S. trade balance had been protected by the more rapid inflation in other countries. The U.S. persistent general price rise was, for a number of reasons, not yet matched by a rise in its export prices. Its exports included certain agricultural products and manufactures whose prices rose less than the average. Moreover, many firms sold their products at lower prices abroad because of differences in demand conditions, or foreign competition, or an eagerness to open new markets. ("Double-pricing" of this kind is quite common in international trade. The tourist is often surprised to find he can buy abroad products manufactured in his own country more cheaply than he could at home, or that he can buy foreign products more cheaply at home.)

Ultimately, of course, export prices rise in response to ever-mounting domestic costs. Meanwhile, export supplies are probably reduced: why sell at lower prices abroad if domestic demand is strong and domestic prices for the same products are rising rapidly? Real trouble for the balance of payments comes when the firm no longer has a choice: rising costs compel charging foreigners more, even if it means losing important customers. Exports inevitably fall.

To return to the United States balance of payments in the years before 1970–71: imports were rising, but so were exports. In the 1950s the U.S. trade surplus had been more than offset by other items in the balance of payments — such as net military expenditures abroad and capital flows; this resulted in an overall deficit. Most regarded this with equanimity. Wasn't the United States improving the external financial position of other countries by redistributing the world's gold reserves in their favor and by building up their holdings of U.S. dollars? Indeed, for these very reasons, the U.S. balance-of-payments deficit was taken as a sign of the success of U.S. policy. The idea that countries abroad would complain that they had too many dollars in their monetary reserves was seen as something that could happen only in Switzerland, a country that had always been suspicious of holding too much of any foreign currency. For the rest, it was just too silly to even suggest this.

Similarly, in the 1950s the ability of the U.S. government to honor its commitment, to cover U.S. dollars officially held abroad into gold at $35 per ounce was not questioned. Then, the U.S. gold stock was adequate to meet this commitment. To expect that monetary authorities outside the United States would wish to convert more than a small fraction of their U.S. dollar acquisitions into gold was unreasonable. U.S. dollars were just as good as gold to meet balance-of-payments deficits; moreover, when the dollars were not used — which was most of the time — they could be invested safely in U.S. interest-earning government obligations. Gold earned nothing — and even cost something to be stored and safeguarded. Central banks outside of the United States could readily dispose of any dollars they acquired to their own citizens and did not feel the need to hold more gold; commercial banks and private firms were eager to build up their cash positions in dollars. This view, while it may seem naïve to some today, was based on the reality of the strength and size of the U.S. economy, and on the felt need of countries around the world to increase their holdings of U.S. dollars for official purposes (monetary reserves) and for business's working balances (private holdings).

Some had, however, argued as early as the 1940s that the United States should change the price of gold — say to $50 or even more per ounce. This would have increased the value of U.S. gold holdings in terms of dollars. However, the principal beneficiaries of such a move would have been South Africa and the U.S.S.R., the world's two leading gold producers. Both countries, for different reasons, were not popular in the United States; for many years, it was the hostility to the U.S.S.R. that was decisively important.

But other arguments were marshaled. Since the gold stock of the United States was considered more than adequate at $35 per ounce and gold production was increasing, why increase its dollar value? By increasing the price of gold, the value of the dollar in terms of gold automatically declined. As a result, holders of dollars would be penalized; they had shown their confidence in the United States by holding such dollars instead of gold, and as the years went on, easing the problems of the United States in this way. Moreover, once done, a change in the U.S. dollar price of gold would bring into question the future value of the dollar in terms of gold, thereby removing a fixed point in the international system — the U.S. official dollar price for gold. In any case, countries outside the United States were financing their balance-of-payments deficits with dollars and sterling, not gold; and substantial outflows of dollars deriving from the continuing U.S. deficit made this task all the easier.

Those who argued for an increase in the gold price did so because they believed that the gold price had not risen while all other prices and costs of gold production had. In real terms, therefore, gold was undervalued. A "realistic" price for gold would stimulate gold production even more; the monetary reserves of the world would automatically be increased in dollar terms and more gold would be forthcoming in the future from increased production.

The lack of concern with U.S. balance-of-payments deficits, indeed, the eagerness to increase foreign holdings of gold and dollars was basic to the decision to put the Marshall Plan's assistance to Europe on a grant basis. No one wanted to re-create the pre–World War II external debt problem by making Europe borrow billions for reconstruction of war damage. That the U.S. was forgoing future repayments on such loans, which would have helped avoid future U.S. balance-of-payments deficits, was not regarded as important. A persistent U.S. balance-of-payments deficit was virtually inconceivable!

The key problem in the postwar period was believed by many to be the "permanent dollar shortage"; that is, not only would there be a lack of sufficient dollar holdings by countries and firms abroad, but also the likelihood was that the U.S. balance of payments would continue to be in surplus. If so, other countries would be chronically short of dollars. Grants rather than loans from the United States would alleviate this situation; dollars would not be needed to service such debts to the United States. It is ironic that this enlightened, if erroneous, view was applied principally to the industrialized countries. By the time aid to the low-income countries came into the center of the international stage in the 1960s, this extraordinarily generous attitude had largely disappeared.

By the 1960s, this optimistic view of the U.S. balance of payments began to change and it became clear that U.S. export prices were rising markedly and many exports were losing their competitiveness. The trend of rising export prices actually began in the 1950s. Starting in 1954–55, even after the inflationary effects of the Korean war of 1950–53 had worn off, U.S. export prices climbed and kept on doing so. There was, however, a slight decline during 1962 and 1963; by 1964, export prices slightly exceeded their 1961 level. Without persistent inflation, U.S. export prices, particularly for manufacturers, might well have declined, reflecting among other things the 3 to 4 percent a year productivity gains of the U.S. economy, and U.S. exports would have risen much more. Reflecting the U.S. inflation in demand and prices, United States imports rose sharply. By 1969, even the trade surplus of previous years had vanished; by 1971 and 1972, a U.S. trade deficit had become a fact of life. To turn the trade position from deficit to surplus was a relatively "new" goal for U.S. economic policy.

The United States was no longer shielded by persistent inflation abroad; its own persistent inflation had finally escalated to a point where it exceeded that elsewhere. A large external trade deficit opened up, paradoxically during a period of relative recession, when it might have been expected (under noninflationary conditions) that American industry would push exports abroad, reducing its demand for imported materials and gaining larger shares of its own domestic markets. Falling imports are the normal consequence of stagnating domestic demand. Instead, in 1970–71, imports were far greater than might have been expected in light of existing economic trends. The trade deficit itself was thus a sign of inflation. And its very presence strengthened inflationary expectations with all their repercussions domestically and internationally. It was this which convinced many that the dollar had become weak. The unfavorable slump in the trade balance broke the camel's back — the U.S. economy as well as the U.S. dollar was now regarded as weak. This fundamental change in the trade picture, even more than the huge outflow of funds in 1971, shook confidence in the future of the U.S. economy and the U.S. currency.

Unless the implications of this course of events are seen, the significance of persistent inflation remains underrated. In other circumstances one might have argued that the U.S. ought to have an external trade deficit: as the most advanced industrial country, with the largest domestic demand, as the largest creditor of foreign countries and firms, and the largest investor abroad, the United States would see its large imports and trade deficit as helping to satisfy its own strong domestic demand and helping other countries to service debts and pay dividends and royalties on U.S. investments. Such behavior internationally might well be expected of a "mature creditor" country. Under ordinary circumstances the U.S. trade deficit would then reflect the combined impacts of fundamental transformation in the U.S. economy and in other economies. Deficits are not, in themselves, signs of weakness. Increases in short-term liabilities to foreigners, represented by increases in their holdings of U.S. dollars, are more than balanced by U.S. increases in income-earning foreign assets. But under prevailing conditions the U.S. deficit was instead seen as a consequence of a weakening in the competitive position of the United States, a weakening brought about by inflation. It strengthened fears of holding U.S. dollars by people outside of the United States. It paralleled the reactions of people in the United States who are acting to defend themselves against a depreciating currency.

It is hard to gauge precisely how much of the change in the U.S balance of payments was due to persistent inflation and how much to other factors like the changing composition of imports, e.g., an increasing proportion being final manufactures. For a number of years, imports into the United States have accounted for a rising percentage of national income or output, from about 3 percent in the mid-1960s to about 4 percent in 1971. This may seem small, but in an economy of the size of the United States', 1 percent is equal to $10 billion per year. Manufactures have grown increasingly significant in such imports. It may well be that imports would have risen, in quantity, even without persistent inflation; but undoubtedly the rise would have been much less and export growth would have been much larger.

The fact that the relative rate of inflation was greater in the United States after the mid-1960s than in a number of other industrial countries worked in the same direction, increasing imports and decreasing exports by erosion of international price competitiveness. It has been estimated that between 1966 and 1971 the U.S. balance of payments deteriorated by about $9 billion for reasons which are attributable not to differences in business conditions (so-called "cyclical" behavior) between the United States and other countries, but to other factors like weakened competitiveness.

Hidden Costs of Persistent Inflation

The balance-of-payments and real-income costs of persistent inflation may be hidden in many ways. In the United States, they were, as we have seen, hidden for many years by the trade surplus; not until this surplus disappeared did it become obvious to some that the U.S. external position had fundamentally weakened. Until then, it could be quite correctly pointed out that special factors — major commercial transactions or military expenditures abroad — accounted for existing deficits. Even now, there is not sufficient recognition that the U.S. balance-of-payments position deteriorated because of persistent inflation and that U.S. surpluses would have been greater without that inflation.

Persistent inflation can be disguised by equivalent or greater inflation taking place in other countries, especially competitors, because the balance-of-payments signals become too weak. Nevertheless, real-income loss in any country still comes from the distortions in consumption and investment, from the social and political effects of the uneven impact of persistent inflation on the distribution of income, and from the uneven ability to defend against this impact. The balance of payments may appear all right because it is not in deficit, or otherwise remains manageable. The facts that real incomes in inflating countries would be higher if inflation were eliminated, and that international trade and the benefits it yields would be greater are neither obvious nor measurable; but this does not make them less real. A crippled man may be able to outrun other crippled men; none of them know how fast they could run if they were not crippled, but most certainly they could run faster.

For years, inflation in other countries made the U.S. inflation appear "small" by contrast. There was also the widespread conviction that some continuing price rise in the United States was needed to avoid higher unemployment —

that it was well worth the cost. The more rapid price increases outside the United States seemed to make it unnecessary to probe deeply into the validity of this thesis, particularly as other countries had lower unemployment rates. Not until more rapid price rises combined with balance-of-payments difficulties did the United States, like other countries, begin to probe more deeply into its own inflationary situation — and then not deeply enough, because the focal point of attention was too often the balance of payments alone.

Achievement of acceptable rates of unemployment and growth without creating inflation and balance-of-payments difficulties is not easy at best. But to do this in an environment that is already inflationary requires a major overhaul of existing national policies, priorities, and institutions. Unless there is a widespread conviction that the problem is serious enough to warrant drastic sustained action to end inflationary expectations and prevent their recurrence, any effort is not likely to succeed.

19

The International Monetary System in the 1950s and 1960s

Parallel to its disruptive effects on any one country's external position, persistent inflation in a number of countries disrupts international monetary and trading arrangements. This problem became increasingly acute and apparent during the 1960s.

In general, the post–World War II world has operated within the so-called Bretton Woods system briefly described in Chapter 6. Under this system, exchange rates are agreed upon internationally in the International Monetary Fund. They can be changed at the initiative of member countries, when the country's balance-of-payments situation has changed in some fundamental way. Only the United States actually undertook the obligation to buy and sell gold to monetary authorities in other countries (*not* to its own citizens) at $35 per ounce. The United States never changed its "parity" because this would involve changing the price at which it bought and sold gold — the focal point of the whole system.

The method of changing the relation between the U.S. dollar and other currencies was regarded as virtually immutable in the 1950s and 1960s. The United States would, as every Secretary of the Treasury after World War II had pledged, simply refuse to change the price of gold. If, as was deemed highly unlikely, the U.S. were to change the price of gold, it was generally believed that other countries would simply change the gold equivalent of their currencies proportionately, restoring the same relative values for their currencies in terms of U.S. dollars. In effect, the system of exchange rates would return to where it had been before the change in the gold price. The key role of the United States resulted simply from the fact that no other country was prepared to undertake the commitment to buy and sell gold in unlimited quantities at a fixed price. The willingness of the United States to do so, however reluctantly fulfilled in practice, explained why foreign central banks held U.S. dollars as international monetary reserves. These dollars could "always" be converted into gold at a known fixed price.

The par-value system combines certainty and flexibility. Certainty comes from the requirement that these par values can only be changed to cope with lasting relative changes in a country's international monetary position, and nearly all such changes require international approval. The need for international approval may give nations, particularly industrial ones, pause as they consider exchange-rate changes. When the change has to be defended before an international body, the country may well hesitate to suggest a change that gives it unfair competitive advantage. Flexibility comes from the fact that any country can initiate a change in its par value and can reasonably expect that the other countries (as they virtually always have) will agree to the proposed change.

The 1950s

Until the last years of the 1950s, the international monetary system functioned quite efficiently with a minimum of squeaks — whether measured by the avoidance of prolonged and severe recessions or the achievement of satisfactory growth rates. It coped quickly and efficiently with balance-of-payments difficulties of industrial members. The steady decline in the U.S. gold holdings in the 1950s was welcomed during most of the next decade. Similarly, almost all welcomed their increased holding of dollars. The U.S. policy of maintaining the gold price of $35 per ounce seemed reasonable from the viewpoint of the structure of exchange rates. Economically, the U.S. was judged basically sound and other industrial countries were growing satisfactorily, partly as a consequence of the massive outflows of U.S. capital and technology.

The move to convertibility of currencies by the European countries at the end of 1958 climaxed this period of progress. This meant that henceforth the European currencies could be used freely and without significant limits to obtain other currencies needed to make international payments for "current" purposes, predominantly trade. The ability of these countries' residents to obtain U.S. dollars in exchange for their own currencies or for others for most purposes was no longer restricted. The limitations, placed at the end of the war by these governments on their residents obtaining U.S. dollars, had resulted in more severe restrictions in buying from the United States and other countries in the "dollar area" — mostly countries in the Western Hemisphere — than in buying imports from non-dollar countries. "Dollar discrimination" had increasingly become a sore point in U.S. economic and political relations with non-dollar countries. Led by the International Monetary Fund, the move to convertibility at the end of 1958 eliminated the financial reasons for this dollar discrimination.

However, convertibility also meant opening economies more to the possibility of balance-of-payments difficulties; people were now freer to import or make other international payments and to move funds from one country to another. To increase the ability of the International Monetary Fund to help countries finance temporary balance-of-payments deficits without going back to severe controls, the size of its pool of currencies was increased by 50 percent in 1959.

In 1962, again to ensure that the international monetary system would have adequate resources and, more particularly, that the Fund would be able to finance larger transactions, ten industrial countries which were members of the Fund, including the United States, the United Kingdom, Canada, France, Germany, Italy, and Japan, agreed to the General Arrangements to Borrow. Financially these Arrangements provided the Fund with facilities to borrow $6 billion in the currencies of the ten countries, on specified conditions, to forestall or to cope with an impairment of the international monetary system. In view of later developments, the reasons given for obtaining these supplementary resources are noteworthy. Convertibility of the main currencies had stimulated international trade and movements of capital; it had at the same time made possible substantial shifts of funds from one country to another. The United States was to be ready to provide $2 billion of these dollar resources — no strong hint yet that some central bank authorities might not wish to accumulate dollars! There was, however, increasing concern with the strength of the international monetary system's ability to cope simultaneously with balance-of-payments deficits in more than one major industrial country, particularly when one of them was the United States.

Signs of Uncertainty: The Later Years

Thus, a relatively new factor was beginning to be felt in international monetary affairs, one which was destined to become of overwhelming importance. As early as 1958, some had ceased regarding the U.S. balance-of-payments deficit with equanimity. By 1960 it was clear that members of the monetary system wanted the deficit eliminated; but, as clearly, this was not going to be easily accomplished. Various measures were taken to reduce the deficit — in the field of U.S. military expenditures abroad, for example — but it continued.

It is essential, however, to an understanding of the events of the 1960s to recall that it was generally believed, in the U.S. and elsewhere, that the U.S. balance-of-payments deficit not only could be brought to an end, but that it could be done without changing the fixed price of gold of $35 per ounce and without ending the commitment of the United States to buy and sell gold to monetary authorities abroad at that price. The elimination of the deficit could be accomplished through a proper combination of fiscal and monetary policies, by so-called demand management. There was some feeling that certain currencies were somewhat undervalued; indeed, in 1961 small revaluations were made by Germany and the Netherlands. But these changes were not regarded as preludes to a change in the official U.S. dollar price for gold.

During the last years of the 1950s, steps had been taken to expand the supply of gold in the London gold market which provided the needs or wishes of industrial and other private users or hoarders of gold. The supply was, however, not sufficient to meet the increased demands which came primarily from continental European central banks as they converted some of their dollar balances into gold. Hoarding and speculative demand by firms and individuals increased the pressures. The dollar price of gold bullion in the London gold market during 1959 and 1960 was usually above the U.S. Treasury selling price. Just before the inauguration of President-elect Kennedy, there was a strong speculative movement which reflected erroneous guesses that the new U.S. administration would change the price of gold. A U.S. executive order, dated January 14, 1961, prohibited the purchase and holding of gold outside the United States by U.S. private citizens and U.S.-owned corporations. Other steps were also taken to reduce speculation in gold, to give central banks additional attractive ways to hold U.S. dollars, and to enable the U.S. monetary authorities to exercise influence in foreign-exchange markets on the exchange rate for U.S. dollars. The last was done by buying and selling foreign currencies provided under short-term borrowing facilities extended by outside central banks: the so-called "swap arrangements."

The magnitude of dollar balances held by monetary authorities abroad in the early 1960s approached that of the total gold holdings of the U.S.; they became equal in 1964 at about $15 billion. Legally, all these dollars could be sold to the United States for gold if the monetary authorities holding them so desired. Increasingly attention focused on how central banks outside of the United States should or would react to the steady growth in their dollar holdings. Some countries, like Canada and Japan, chose to hold dollars; others, like the U.K., continued for some years to hold their reserves substantially in gold; others (Germany, for example) tended to divide their accumulation of monetary reserves between gold and dollars.

Some central bankers were beginning to voice alarm. The U.S. administration also began to show increasing concern with these holdings; from its point of view, they were liabilities — potential claims on the U.S. gold stock. The U.S. gold stock was still the largest in the world, but after 1965 it was no longer large enough to meet all possible demands for conversion into gold of dollars held by monetary authorities outside the United States.

Indeed, the U.S. overall balance-of-payments deficit was not as large as special external U.S. government expenditures, e.g., defense and foreign aid, which amounted to about $3 to $4 billion per year. Moreover, its trade accounts still showed an impressively large surplus. If necessary, special arrangements (like offsetting military procurement in the United States by the Allied Nations) could compensate for these sources of deficit. By 1964, the official outlook for the U.S. balance of payments was favorable; it was believed that confidence in the U.S. dollar was again increasing.

The U.S. did not use the credit facilities of the Interna-

tional Monetary Fund to help finance its deficits because
other mechanisms for this were still viable — and use of the
Fund might be taken as a sign of weakness. Most important
was the willingness, however reluctant, of countries to hold
more dollars. The cooperation among central banks, in the
form of swap arrangements, grew from its inception in 1961,
and operated with remarkable efficiency. The U.S. acted as
though it were convinced that its underlying external position was strong and that the deficit would be brought to an
end in a relatively short span of time. Much was made of the
fact that rates of inflation were more rapid in other industrial
countries. The limitations placed in 1964 on U.S. direct
investments abroad were claimed to be temporary. Therefore, although the U.S. administration was by this time
greatly concerned about its external deficit and eager to
avoid further gold losses, there was no pressure to bring
about important revaluations of other major currencies in
order to strengthen the U.S. balance-of-payments position.
The $35 price for gold remained firm policy. And the U.S.
continued to be a major source of assistance to other countries, particularly to the U.K., in meeting their balance-of-
payments difficulties.

Whether the confidence felt in the first part of the 1960s
that the U.S. could bring its balance of payments into sustained equilibrium, or close to equilibrium, was justified, will
remain debatable, though it was surely an optimistic view.
By 1964, signs that the U.S. balance of payments was improving markedly were visible. However, acceleration of
the war in Vietnam strengthened inflationary pressures in the
United States as fiscal policies did not cope with the heightened levels of demand.

The higher rate of U.S. inflation in the latter part of the 1960s reinforced already growing inflationary expectations. Both in the U.S. and in other countries, accelerating U.S. inflation became accepted as likely and as a basis for policy making. Increasingly, new interpretations derogatory to the United States economy were given to the strengthening of inflationary pressures and the continued balance-of-payments deficits. For the first time since the end of World War II, serious and widespread questions were raised about the international competitiveness of the U.S. economy and the ability of the United States to end its deficits. The wisdom of holding U.S. dollar assets was called into question, not on the grounds that holding gold was preferable because there might be a change in the price of gold (as favored by some countries despite the insistence of the U.S. authorities to the contrary), but rather on the grounds that a change in the price of gold was inevitable in view of persistent and now quite rapid U.S. inflation. There were even those who had begun to speculate seriously as to whether the U.S. could keep the dollar linked to gold, and many publicly expressed the view that the U.S. would need to move to a floating exchange-rate system terminating the link to gold.

All these developments were mutually reinforcing. How would public officials outside the U.S. justify holding even larger amounts of U.S. dollars in the face of these adverse developments? The argument that these dollar accumulations resulted from the inflationary pressures created by the Vietnam war did not make countries more eager to hold them. Political views became mingled with economic and monetary considerations. To the monetary authorities who held dollars in central banks and treasuries or ministries of finance, the risk inherent in their doing so became increasingly apparent, particularly as the price of gold went up in gold markets. Defensive measures were taken. Efforts were made to retain gold as a vital part of the international monetary system, despite the ever-growing demand for gold for all sorts of purposes in addition to monetary reserves; countries cooperated to prevent leakages from their monetary reserves into those speculative gold markets. But the defensive measures proved to be too weak. The decisive reason for their failure was, I believe, the spreading strong conviction that the rapid inflation in the United States made its currency a poor international reserve asset.

The Formation of SDRs

All during this period, ever-mounting international liquidity created by the U.S. balance-of-payments deficit contrasted with ongoing discussions of future sources of international liquidity — discussion carried on in the expectation, or at least hope, of reversal of the U.S. balance-of-payments position.

Discussions began in earnest on the so-called "liquidity problem" in the mid-1960s. The "liquidity problem" merits some explanation. Countries have various ways to deal with their balance-of-payments deficits. One is to finance them by using accumulated monetary reserves held by their central banks — mostly U.S. dollars, gold, or sterling. These reserves are the country's international liquidity, just as a firm's cash holdings or bank deposits are its liquidity. Globally, the only major fast-growing component in international monetary reserves had been U.S. dollars resulting from the continuing U.S. deficits. If this source of monetary reserves were dried up because the U.S. deficit ceased, the monetary reserves which provided the "liquidity" to finance deficits of countries would also cease to grow. At the same time, balance-of-payments deficits could be expected to be ever larger, even if temporary, because international trade was itself growing. At higher levels of imports and exports, changes in either could mean larger deficits. Therefore unfavorable external developments would be expressed in ever-larger money terms. At these new levels, global reserves would be inadequate. This "liquidity problem" was thought the likely result of the elimination of the U.S. dollar deficit as a major source of additional liquidity. With inadequate liquidity, the new and rising levels of world output, employment, and foreign trade would be jeopardized; countries would have to reduce imports if they faced balance-of-payments difficulties with inadequate reserves. The U.S. external deficit, though it had lasted for years, was still regarded in 1964 as temporary and reversible; surpluses were expected and were feared by some! Nine years later, these surpluses have yet to appear.

With the short-lived cessation of significant increases in the world's monetary reserves in the latter part of the 1960s, the stage was set for the introduction, in 1970, of a scheme in the IMF for Special Drawing Rights — SDRs. They are "Special" Drawing Rights to distinguish them from the "ordinary" drawing rights in the Fund. These SDRs or, as they are frequently referred to, "paper gold," gave Fund members additional international assets to finance balance-of-payments deficits and in which to hold monetary reserves. Like paper money, they are simply created by the actions of governments. Their usability comes from their acceptability by governments as means of settling international debts. Special Drawing Rights were seen as a mechanism to replace the world's reliance on U.S. dollar deficits for increases in liquidity. Countries would, presumably, no longer have any vested interest in the continuation of U.S. deficits because such deficits increased their monetary reserves.

The further decline during this period in the international reserve role of sterling was increasingly taken as a harbinger of what was bound to happen to the dollar — if the U.S. economy could not overcome inflation and sustain a satisfactory balance-of-payments position. The dollar would decline in this important international monetary role, as happened in the case of the pound sterling.

Euro-Currency Market

Another major development of the 1960s is quite pertinent to an understanding of today's conditions: the dramatic evolution of the Euro-dollar or Euro-currency market into a major element in the international monetary system. In 1963, the U.S. had imposed an "interest equalization tax," a tax on foreign longer-term borrowing in the United States, to discourage such borrowing. Exemptions were made for low-income countries. In addition, various measures — voluntary restraints and controls over direct investments and lending abroad by American business and financial institutions — were introduced. With these limitations on financial transactions in the United States, London and other European centers became much more important as mobilizers of world savings for relending to credit-worthy borrowers anywhere. In this truly international money and capital market, the supply of foreign exchange — initially, mostly dollars — resulted from economic activities in all parts of the world: oil revenues from the Middle East, capital flight from Latin America, European central banks eager to find some use for their mounting dollar balances, branches of U.S. firms wishing to escape limitations on direct foreign investments, and American banks eager to profit from the lively business in Europe. All these provided deposits, mostly in dollars but also in other currencies. Euro-deposits virtually soared, and now (1973) they are estimated at about $100 billion. Interest rates and other terms of international borrowing increasingly now tend to follow the lead given in the Euro-currency market.

The Euro-currency market made it possible for firms in the United States and elsewhere to look to London and other European centers to provide financing, not only for international transactions, but also to meet domestic financial needs arising out of domestic credit policies or institutional limitations. Of course this was not an entirely new phenomenon; however, the ease of transaction and the magnitudes which the Euro-dollar market was prepared to handle transformed international financial relations. Banking and other financial institutions were developing the sophistication to deal with their multinational counterparts in the industrial and trading world. A world-wide corporation could seek world-wide capital to meet its financial needs: the demand for, as well as the supply of, funds was truly global. It was one of the fruits of the move to convertibility.

With these developments, management of the international monetary situation as well as of domestic monetary conditions had also become more complicated. Both international inflows and outflows of funds were increasingly sensitive to changes in credit conditions in the major industrial countries, and to the possibilities of changes in their exchange rates. As countries found the pursuit of flexible fiscal policies to be very difficult in trying to manage their domestic affairs, they relied heavily on monetary policy; but the dangers of large international flows of funds induced by interest differentials was constantly present. Why hold money at 6 percent interest in the U.S., if it could earn 8 percent in Europe? The international credit-rating of countries and firms could be measured by how much more (sometimes less) they had to pay for loans than prime borrowers in the Euro-currency market. Monetary authorities came to use the Euro-currency market to help manage their domestic monetary situations and their balances of payments. It was a market in which to dispose of excess dollar acquisitions, or borrow dollars, if needed, or in which to permit firms to borrow for their own domestic purposes if credit got too tight at home.

An Evaluation

On balance, the international monetary system worked reasonably well in the 1950s and, in many respects, even during much of the 1960s. World trade continued to expand at sustained rates without historical precedents. High growth rates were achieved in many countries. Unemployment was not a serious problem in the industrial countries. The world did not return to the Great Depression of the 1930s. Thus, the system fulfilled those fundamental criteria which dominated thinking leading to the Bretton Woods Agreement in 1944. Unemployment was increasing in the developing countries but this seemed more related to deficiencies in development strategies than to weaknesses in the international monetary system. The basic weakness of the system was its failure, in the developed and developing countries, to make persistent inflation impossible. Though this weakness was there for many years, it did not lead to a general breakdown of the agreed rules among the developed countries. Simultaneous inflation in these countries postponed the inevitable collapse. In the developing countries, persistent and higher rates of inflation meant that they had to be, and were, excused from living by the agreed rules of stable exchange rates and avoidance of restrictions on international payments. Exceptions for these countries, however, did not affect importantly the functioning of the international system.

20

The Events of 1971 and After

Breakdown in 1971

The system finally broke down in 1971. Major industrial countries changed their exchange rates — but they did not do so in the manner agreed on in the rules of the International Monetary Fund. In May 1971, Germany decided to "float" the Deutschmark; to allow the demand and supply in the foreign-exchange market to determine the foreign value of the German mark currency, rather than to fix a new parity with the Fund. Canada had taken similar action in the 1950s, but Canada was not as important economically as Germany. The floating of the Canadian dollar was not taken as a precedent for the developed countries: Canada's extraordinarily close economic and financial relations with the United States provided a rationale for regarding its action as exceptional. Germany wanted to raise the value of — to "revalue" — its currency, a step it took out of fear of domestic inflation. Revaluation would tend to discourage exports and encourage imports, thereby tending to reduce the German balance-of-payments surplus. By achieving these ends, revaluation would improve the ability of the government to combat inflation and, more particularly, to act against a rise in wages of such magnitude as would accelerate the wage-price spiral. Other countries — the Netherlands, Austria, and Switzerland — also revalued, but only Austria did so by declaring a new par value with the Fund.

A more devastating blow to the existing international system of rules was dealt in August 1971. On August 15, 1971, the President of the United States announced, as part of the New Economic Policy, the suspension of the convertibility of the United States dollar into gold: the U.S. ceased buying or selling gold. By this action President Nixon ended the Bretton Woods era in international monetary relations.

We entered an era of transition. How "new" or "changed" the future international monetary system will be remains to be seen. For some weeks after President Nixon suspended the convertibility of the dollar into gold, the exchange rates of major currencies were determined in exchange markets largely by the interplay of supply and demand. Monetary authorities exercised their own judgments as to appropriate policies to influence the level of their exchange rates. The consequences were great uncertainty and large speculative international movements of funds.

Smithsonian Meeting

In December 1971, a meeting was held at the Smithsonian Institution in Washington which was intended to end uncertainty and the resultant disorder of exchange markets; it was to pave the way for thoughtful and careful reform of the existing monetary system. The ministers and governors of the ten countries that attended issued a communiqué stating that they had agreed to "an interrelated set of measures designed to restore stability to international monetary arrangements and to provide for expanding international trade." They expressed the hope that all governments would cooperate through the Fund to permit the implementation of these measures "in an orderly fashion." They also reached agreement on the pattern of exchange-rate relationships among their ten currencies. No country, they stressed, should seek "improper competitive advantage through its exchange policies." But the new rates would have a greater range than the old: central banks had to intervene if the rate rose or fell 2.25 percent, not 1 percent as before, from its central value.

The United States agreed to propose to its Congress a suitable means for devaluing the dollar in terms of gold to $38 per ounce, at such time as the results of short-term trade negotiations were "available for Congressional scrutiny." Once the required legislative authority had been obtained, the United States undertook to propose a corresponding new par value of the dollar to the International Monetary Fund. The 10 percent surcharge on many imported goods which the U.S. had imposed as part of its New Economic Policy was immediately suspended.

Although the agreement reached at the Smithsonian meeting did not result formally in a new price for gold — Congressional action was necessary before this could happen — it was clearly assumed that the U.S. dollar had depreciated by the anticipated increase of 8.57 percent in the price of gold. (Subsequently, the U.S. Congress did act and a new

U.S. par value was established.) Those countries which maintained their par values appreciated their currencies by that amount against the U.S. dollar.

Even more significant was the agreement that discussions should be promptly undertaken, particularly in the framework of the International Monetary Fund, to consider reform of the international monetary system. In effect the agenda for these discussions was set forth in the Smithsonian communiqué: "It was agreed that attention should be directed to the appropriate monetary means and division of responsibilities for defending stable exchange rates and for ensuring a proper degree of convertibility of the system; to the proper role of gold, of reserve currencies, and of Special Drawing Rights in the operation of the system; to the appropriate volume of liquidity; to re-examination of the permissible margins of fluctuation around established exchange rates and other means of establishing a suitable degree of flexibility; and to other measures dealing with movements of liquid capital. It is recognized that decisions in each of these areas are closely linked."

After this meeting, the International Monetary Fund announced its adoption of a decision to establish a temporary regime of exchange rates; in effect, this permitted members to act in accordance with the Smithsonian agreement. The new exchange value for a currency resulting from this realignment, if it were only for the purpose of this temporary regime rather than a new par value, was to be referred to as a "central rate." Some countries — France and the United Kingdom, Australia, New Zealand, and Spain — chose to keep their par values unchanged, in effect revaluing their currencies in terms of U.S. dollars. Some countries — among them Tanzania and Uganda — took the occasion to appreciate their currencies so that they remained unchanged in terms of dollars. Others — such as Yugoslavia and South Africa — took advantage of the occasion to bring about major devaluations of their currencies in terms of dollars.

Many more countries in effect took the third alternative indicated in the Group of Ten communiqué; instead of maintaining or changing their par value, they chose to establish central rates. However, among the countries that established central rates, there were great differences as to the changes made in their currencies in terms of U.S. dollars. Belgium, Luxembourg, and the Netherlands established central rates which represented effective revaluations of 11.5 percent in the par value of their currencies in terms of U.S. dollars. Germany and Japan effectively revalued by 13.58 and 16.88 percent, respectively. Other countries made changes that were considerably less; for example, Italy revalued by 7.48 percent, Sweden by 7.49 percent, and Portugal, 5.50 percent.

These differences in changes pointed to major issues in currency policies. The European countries feared Japanese competition and wanted Japan to revalue its currency, the yen, more than the European currencies. Within Europe, German competition was feared more than others'. The changes made weakened the competitive position of Japan and Germany vis-à-vis other countries as well as the United States.

Thus, the first half of 1972 saw a world-wide major realignment of exchange rates. The average devaluation of the

U.S. dollar has been estimated at about 10 to 11 percent. Despite these actions, the U.S. balance-of-payments deficit has continued, and central banks outside the United States continued to accumulate dollars. In terms of foreign-exchange operations, the exchange rates of industrial countries prevailing in foreign-exchange markets seemed more realistic by the summer of 1972 than they had been for some time. It remains to be seen, however, how enduring this pattern of exchange rates will prove to be.

The changes made represented critical departures from the international monetary system. The most important was that the established legal link between dollars and gold has been greatly weakened, if not permanently broken, and an international reserve currency was not living by the rules. Certain temporary devices have been agreed to, but much remains different in practice as well as in principle. On the other hand, certain important features of the system were preserved and a more realistic and more flexible pattern of exchange rates was achieved. Nonetheless, the viability of the exchange-rate mechanism was put in doubt, and a crucial but most difficult problem is to agree on a new set of rules which will command respect and restore confidence to the system — an objective that may well prove impossible to achieve in an environment of persistent world-wide inflation.

Lessons of History

A new international monetary system has yet to be designed or, as may well happen, simply to evolve from a series of events. The events of the year 1971–72 particularly drove home certain other lessons which are bound greatly to affect future deliberations on the international monetary system. Perhaps most important is that any international monetary system must be based on a pattern of exchange rates which is realistic by objective economic criteria; it must be capable of achieving satisfactory balance-of-payments positions without forcing countries to resort to the widespread use of restrictions on current payments. Equally important, the pattern of rates must be regarded as realistic. Without this confidence, speculation will exacerbate balance-of-payments difficulties to the point of forcing recourse to restrictions or exchange-rate changes which are otherwise unnecessary.

The United States did not have to face devaluation of its currency as long as budgetary deficits could be attributed to temporary factors such as the Korean war, or to different timing in the phases of the U.S. business cycle compared with others, or even to the prolonged Vietnam war. The more rapid pace of inflation over a period of years led to the conviction that the deficit in the trade account in 1971 was not temporary. Rather, it was "fundamental." Most important for this was the trade deficit, the first since World War II. Even further increases in dollar liabilities as compared with gold need not have had the consequences of devaluation.

It is, of course, impossible to say what amounts of dollar liabilities might, given noninflationary conditions, have been piled on a given gold base. What is clear is that persistent inflation, particularly at a rate higher than that of other industrial countries, toppled the pile. The U.S. dollar ex-

change rate was no longer credible. The lesson here is that
the world pattern of exchange rates, particularly among the
major industrial countries, has to be kept under review and
adjusted as conditions warrant. This is one reason for further strengthening the machinery of international consultation. Clearly, too, the mechanism for changing exchange
rates needs to be made more flexible and, if possible, less
obstructed by governmental difficulties in initiating such
changes. Experience has taught that changes in exchange
rates are major, difficult, political decisions; but this may be
because we believe that to be the case. We may be able to
evolve a system which would facilitate changes in rates when
objective indicators indicated such changes were desirable.
Initiative could be given to the International Monetary
Fund, though in practice the significance of such a step
would depend on the role which governments were prepared
to see the Fund exercise. Different mechanisms are possible.
Critically important is the readiness of the nations of the
world to delegate national sovereignty in this field beyond,
or differently from, the delegation already embodied in the
Fund Articles of Agreement.

Governments must be able to act promptly in changing
exchange rates once the decision to do so has been taken.
Greater flexibility in the mechanism for changing exchange
rates would not obviate the need to have adequate internationally acceptable resources to finance deficits in the balance
of payments — even in a number of countries simultaneously. But if the so-called "adjustment mechanism" is to
operate properly, these resources should not be used to
maintain unrealistic exchange rates. On the other hand,

industrialized countries clearly are not eager to permit competitors to obtain "unfair" advantage by "excessive" devaluations: they are likely to police each other carefully in this respect.

The speed with which the major industrial countries brought to an end conditions prevailing in exchange markets in the latter half of 1971, gives still another lesson. Many countries, e.g., the countries in the Common Market, appeared unwilling to permit the free market to determine their exchange rates and value stability. On the other hand, there was the decision of the United Kingdom to "float" its exchange rate in July 1972. Faced by very strong inflationary pressures, the British decided that the sterling's par value could not be maintained. A high degree of certainty and stability in exchange rates is desirable from the viewpoint of the orderly and efficient conduct of international trade and finance. This is particularly true among countries trying to achieve close economic integration like the Common Market.

The events of the year 1971–72 also demonstrate that any efficient monetary system must be prepared to deal with very large, frequently unpredictable changes in the balance of payments. Deficits caused by such swings, although temporary, may swamp normally available resources; these should not require exchange-rate changes or the forced introduction of governmental restrictions. Mechanisms can be devised to deal with this. The basic need is to assure the future existence of internationally acceptable monetary reserves in adequate amounts and distributed by criteria of genuine need. Some find undesirable any system that permits countries to finance large and persistent balance-of-payments deficits with their own national currencies — as the U.S. and Britain have; they argue, in consequence, the desirability of using only international reserve assets like gold and SDRs. However, there is little point in this argument until such time as countries show willingness to substitute other reserve assets for natural currencies and then their changed role as reserves would not jeopardize the essential role they now play in facilitating international trade and capital movements.

Underlying any decision on the international monetary system will need to be a basic judgment as to whether or not persistent inflation will continue to characterize the domestic economies of the industrialized countries. Whatever the issue — exchange rates, use of governmental controls, or future ties to gold — the answer will be very different depending on that judgment. If the answer is that persistent inflation is likely to continue, the system — if it can truly be called a system — is more likely to be very flexible, avoiding limitations on governments' freedom of domestic action; governments must expect repeated balance-of-payments difficulties and recurrent need for major changes in all the elements of their balance-of-payments management, not only the exchange rate. Under these circumstances, international consultation or supervision becomes very onerous and less meaningful — less meaningful because the frequent need for speedy changes diminishes its effectiveness. Which countries will inflate more than others? Will the inflation offset devaluation? Will the devaluation cause further accleration of inflation, etc? All these — and more — will continue to be uncertainties until the inflation is halted.

Some may suggest that the balance-of-payments effects of

persistent inflation could be offset by international arrangements for automatic changes in exchange rates, as would be
the case with floating exchange rates. This can be done. I
am, however, convinced that the expansion of international
trade is facilitated by certainty in exchange rates. Moreover,
by encouraging the continuation of inflation, such systems
could be very costly to all countries because of the domestic
effects, even if balance-of-payments deficits become less
frequent and more manageable. If persistent inflation is overcome in the years ahead, the need for automatic exchange-
rate-adjustment mechanisms will then be greatly reduced.
Under noninflationary conditions the debate over fluctuating
rates would probably cease to be important.

But should some variant of such schemes gain international
support, its specifications had better be clear and visible, so
that all concerned can anticipate the changes. It will be hard
enough to conduct international trade under such circumstances; all that will be known is that countries experiencing
more inflation than certain others will devalue by amounts
approximately equivalent to the difference between their
rates of inflation and those rates being experienced elsewhere, particularly by their major trading partners. Presumably, devaluation should only be necessary when the
cumulative effect of the differences becomes significant.
This effect need not be as large as hitherto, but also not too
trivial to warrant a change, unless the system is one of
automatic adjustment to any and all differences. With even
the possibility that countries would not devalue, the system
becomes highly unpredictable. Predictability comes from in-
sisting on "realistic" exchange rates — ones which reflect rela-

tive economic positions and achievement of noninflationary conditions in the industrialized countries. The difficulty is how to ensure this in a world of countries not yet ready to surrender their national sovereignty over exchange-rate decisions and not able to end persistent inflation.

Even a system of floating rates does not ensure "realistic" exchange rates. Governments could, if they chose, influence conditions in exchange markets to a very marked degree. The likelihood that governments would not allow their exchange rates to "float" freely is heightened by the fact that export competition can be maintained during periods of inflation by ways other than devaluation.

Solution is not easy. It lies somewhere between two limits. One is the insistence that a country with balance-of-payments difficulties resulting from persistent inflation end the inflation. Until it does, it can neither expect other countries to help finance its deficits nor to tolerate restrictions on imports or other international transactions by the inflating country. Instead, inflating countries must themselves take the brunt of adjustment by devaluing. The other limit is to make exchange-rate change so easy that it encourages governments to perpetuate inflationary policies by eliminating or easing the balance-of-payments consequences. This is the great danger in the use of fluctuating or floating-rate systems.

Those responsible for the design and the management of the international monetary system will have the benefits of post–World War II experiences. Certain lessons are clear. An effective international monetary system is imperative to sustain the expansion of the world economy. It does this at different levels and in many different ways. Within countries, it facilitates the pursuit of modern objectives — high levels of employment, satisfactory growth rates, improved income distribution. At the international level, an effective international monetary system is a prerequisite for expanding international trade and enabling large-scale transfers of private and public capital and technology. Without these, countries would be unable to fulfill their domestic objectives. Economic and social problems would be greatly multiplied.

A well-functioning international monetary system is thus necessary if the world is not to regress to more reliance on measures which contract international trade and flows of capital and technology. Protectionism, in its various forms, has been held at bay for over thirty years, though it still remains important. This helps explain why the world has had a period of unprecedented growth and improvement in material well-being. The postwar growth has created, as we have seen, its own problems. Increased protectionism would have added more problems — domestic and international — and not helped existing ones. We probably would have had even stronger inflationary pressures.

Persistent inflation, among its other corrosive effects, weakens the concern for maintaining an international monetary and trading system. The urgent problems created for countries by this inflation supersede the concern with the harmful effects of a breakdown in the international system. This very situation may explain the monetary crisis in early 1973: inflation rates in Europe and Japan are climbing, not abating; these countries' concerns necessarily have turned inward. Similar practices could also flourish in a period of prolonged unacceptable widespread unemployment. But the Bretton Woods system provided the machinery for coping with those conditions of widespread unemployment. Now, with a fresh start being made in renewing the international monetary system, a similar determination is needed: to build a system which both discourages continuous inflation and makes it difficult for countries to export their inflationary pressures, while it preserves their ability to prevent severe and prolonged depression.

Thus, by the early 1970s we have learned at least two basic principles about the world economy. It cannot survive widespread and prolonged recession. It cannot survive persistent and widespread inflation. In both cases the major industrial countries are the decisive factors. Therefore, an answer must be found to the conundrum of simultaneously achieving both objectives — elimination of persistent inflation and maintenance of full employment. In modern society this cannot be done without also achieving other primary national targets: satisfactory growth rates, social justice, and an improved quality of life. We have failed miserably on too many counts. New approaches must be sought and new solutions tried until we reach the proper mixtures which give us a stronger and more certain basis for sustained progress in the still murky and shoal-strewn future.

International Aspects of a Program of Action

A guide to a program of action to achieve these ends is given subsequently. As for the international economic relations, they should be so organized that the national strategies for overcoming persistent inflation can be assisted as the Bretton

Woods system aided the pursuit of full-employment objectives.

An international system to do this would encourage a higher level of output of goods and services. It would discourage consumerism by encouraging domestic measures to do so and, to the extent possible, cooperating internationally to achieve that end.

It would discourage countries from pursuing inflationary policies by trying to help avoid new inflation, and would eliminate inflationary expectations by enhancing the likelihood of increased supplies from domestic and international sources.

Closely related, it would encourage countries to follow policies which resulted in higher levels of savings, particularly in the developed countries, where even small increases in the proportion of total output saved augment greatly the resources available for investment both in the developed and developing countries.

It would encourage national and international practices which increase competition within and among economies.

It would give due recognition to the needs of lower-income countries for exceptional international treatment such as protective tariffs to encourage new, truly "infant" industries.

It would assist countries to formulate national strategies which would benefit from, but not merely imitate, the experiences and practices of others in reconciling employment, growth, and income-distribution objectives with conservation of exhaustible raw materials, environmental protection, and with the elimination of persistent inflation. Institutions such as the World Bank, the International Monetary Fund, the various regional banks (for example, the Inter-American Development Bank and the Asian Development Bank), various UN bodies, such as the new environmental organization and the International Labor Office, all could help.

They would also assist countries, if assistance were needed, to identify high-priority investments and to help in their execution.

The international system would improve the mechanism for the flow of goods, services, and technology from richer to poorer countries by using private as well as national and international public institutions and by re-examining how they might improve the world's distribution of consumption until such time as the international pattern of income distribution made such measures unnecessary. (This assumes that industrial economies in the meantime will *not* have taken the road of reducing their capacity to produce and become the playground of the higher-income world instead of the workshop of the world.)

The international system would eliminate for developed countries the balance-of-payments justification for limiting the export of productive capital, particularly to the lower-income countries.

It would incorporate the principle of the need of the developing countries for more goods and services from the developed countries as part of the legitimate demands on the developed countries, requiring from them increased efforts to improve their own productive capacities.

Finally, it would include an international monetary system which was firmly grounded on the principle that elimination of persistent inflation and achievement of noninflationary conditions are equal in importance to avoidance of prolonged recession and economic stagnation.

In these ways the international economic system would serve the social as well as economic objectives of modern societies. If it does not do so, it will not be a viable system. If it does, it will, among other benefits, greatly assist the international political efforts to achieve a sustained era of international peace.

VII

Overcoming
Persistent Inflation

21

Guides for Programs
of National Action

Precise programs of action — like precise conclusions —
must be made country by country. A universal program
applicable to all countries — or even a few model programs
deemed applicable to a few broad categories of countries —
could only be simplistic. What follow, therefore, are guidelines, not detailed maps, for use in considering, preparing,
and implementing individual programs of action. These
guides accept as national objectives the pursuit of full employment, reasonable economic growth in the industrial
countries and accelerated growth in the developing countries, and satisfactory improvement in the quality of life,
ranging from more equitable income distribution to environmental improvement in all countries.

The guides to action consist essentially of suggestions for:
(1) obtaining required information and background material on each country; (2) identifying political, social, and
economic problem areas and selection of priorities; (3) choice
among priorities; (4) implementation of these priorities and
formulation of proposals on economic and social management; and (5) recommendations for the use of mechanisms
or institutions to achieve these objectives.

These guides would yield a situation vastly different from today's, but begin with existing institutions. Modern institutions and practices have long histories and therefore adaptation is not easy. But dealing with persistent inflation and with current deep societal problems is one and the same thing. People everywhere are demanding a much more effective attack on these ills. Ideologies and approaches may differ, but the fundamental concern is the same. This makes major innovation in thought and deed both necessary and practical.

(1) Required Information and Knowledge

The information and analyses required to deal effectively with these problems cover many fields. We are essentially in the realm of public policy-making. Such problems simultaneously involve many, if not all, human activities: economics, politics, law, history, sociology, psychology. We have many well-trained and well-disciplined experts, but relatively few equally well-trained and well-disciplined generalists able to learn from many disciplines and make judgments accordingly. Thus, we begin on the task of coping with persistent inflation with a shortage of needed talent. This could, of course, be overcome by on-the-job training. If nothing focuses the mind like the prospect of being hanged, then nothing sharpens the mind like the need to make policy recommendations and decisions and the fact of being held accountable for them.

The information and background material on each country should include the best possible detailed analyses of the society and its economy together with a synthesis of these analyses, showing the interrelations of various parts and activities. This provides the basis for a thoroughgoing understanding in each country of persistent inflation, its strength and significance. For this purpose, a statistical index or indices of inflationary expectations can be formulated based on its various manifestations, many of which have been suggested herein.

In making these analyses, it is more useful for economic and social policy-making to have a rough approximation of reality than a precise delineation of an oversimplified abstraction. By seeing problems in their many important aspects and trying to understand their interrelations, the policies based on this synthesis, though inevitably imperfect, are more likely to meet with success. Policies to eliminate persistent inflation are particularly in need of this sense of reality and its complexities.

A word of caution: the need to tackle these problems cannot await complete or even satisfactory knowledge and the ability to use it well. It is necessary to act with the best available information and judgment, recognizing the need to be flexible, prepared to acknowledge error and change policies, as better understanding is achieved and also in response to changing conditions.

(2) Identification of Problem Areas and Priorities

We need immediate efforts to identify the major social, political, and economic problem areas and to provide the factual basis for obtaining through a process of public debate, a consensus as to which of these problems we are prepared to tackle for the foreseeable future. In many countries problem areas have been identified for other purposes; the knowledge obtained should be most helpful. The selection and implementation of priorities can profit greatly by technical analyses and other technical inputs. But these must not be regarded as technical issues if they are to be publicly understood and dealt with politically.

(3) *Choice Among Priorities*

The need to choose among competing claims on national priorities is now so repeatedly emphasized that despite its fundamental validity it may have lost its public appeal and potency as a policy issue. Often, of course, choices must be made for reasons of short-term political expediency. What is done is by definition the best feasible choice even if it is dead wrong. No amount of prior thinking and planning about national priorities will avoid the repeated necessity of doing the politically expedient and often this will prove to be a "mistake" from the longer-run point of view. However, it is possible to minimize the number of times when costly errors are made. This can be done by having an overall strategic approach to the problem of persistent inflation.

There are many ways to develop such a strategy. In my own experience with countries, the achievement of the elimination of the basic causes of persistent inflation would be greatly helped by viewing the problem as one of "bottlenecks" in society. These "bottlenecks" are the conditions which prevent a society and its economy from attaining desired patterns of behavior.

These desired patterns reflect the society's objectives. Its objectives may well be in dispute, but during any given period, what consensus prevails is reasonably well known. Thus, in the United States today, there is a consensus that unemployment should be low and short-lived, that education through advanced levels should be universally available. Minimum consumption standards, irrespective of earnings, should prevail as should freedom from concern about basic livelihood during old age and illness. Income distribution should be more equitable, with equality in economic and social opportunity for ethnic and racial minorities — and acceptance of such for women. Urban conditions need drastic improvement; the environment requires rehabilitation, and so forth. There is significant disagreement and debate about implementation, but the objectives and purposes can be quite widely recognized. Similar consensuses exist in other countries.

In achieving such purposes, special difficulties arise which are particularly important because until they are overcome further progress becomes nearly impossible. In unemployment, it may be "hard-core" unemployment; in income distribution, it may be resistance to tax increases coupled with resistance to major changes in the structure of taxation; in improving the quality of life, it may be the acceptance of a value system implicit in consumerism or the apparent impossibility of additional large-scale governmental expenditures, at least until others are greatly reduced; in growth, it may be the need to achieve more savings and more capital imports to enable more investment and a better economic management of available resources; in family planning, it may be personal religious attitudes or lack of clinical facilities, and so forth. Experience indicates that it is possible to identify and analyze the "critical" bottlenecks to further progress.

Because there are likely to be more problems than can be tackled simultaneously, priorities must be determined — how much to be done in different areas, in what order, and by what means. In this breaking-of-bottlenecks approach, it would be most welcome, but highly unlikely, if the order of priorities which proved socially and politically acceptable were also the most efficient — yielding the best results for the efforts made. In some countries, it is even dubious whether an ordering of social or economic priorities can be achieved. Public debate sometimes has to wait until government measures, taken on a seemingly ad hoc basis, have their effects. For example, as steps are taken to implement a model urban redevelopment program, or to control some specific pollutant like industrial waste or gasoline, or as busing is used to overcome racial discrimination, the public interest may then be aroused; debate of national priorities might well follow rather than precede, though logic might indicate the opposite.

But governments must select their policies and courses of action on the basis of a value system together with judgments on feasibility. In fact, they do determine and implement priorities. They can direct their efforts toward attacking those social and economic ills which they regard as paramount and practical to attack. If they choose very badly, they will lose the constituency without which modern governments find it most difficult to survive.

As time goes on, the political process will be largely taken up with the choice of these priorities and judgments on how they are being implemented. Bread-and-butter issues have always been very important "political" issues. They will become even more important and vastly increase in number as modern governments try to perform the Herculean tasks of fulfilling their new economic and social responsibilities.

(4) Implementation of Priorities

Need for Overall Strategy: Debate should also seek an overall strategy to attack the fundamental problems of societies and ensure future progress. Such strategies can be realistically framed; they need not be platitudinous or innocuous. They will, no doubt, be highly controversial; the selection of priorities and the instruments chosen for their implementation involve highly charged political and social questions. Nor can they be free from subjective judgments even though details like investment choices can be filled in by objective criteria. Details are very important for the success of any strategy, but prior choices are needed. The job of the political process is to pose the choices; to enable people to choose among them and thereby to provide the needed public support for their implementation, and, where necessary, to help build needed institutions or adapt existing ones.

National Planning and Programming: Many countries have experimented with various forms of national planning or programming to formulate and implement such strategies. Modern "planned" economies, particularly the U.S.S.R., provide outstanding examples. They dictate the details of consumption as well as production, trading and financing in all sectors of the economy. Their "Five-Year Plans" became the prototype for numerous others after World War II, including countries like India where the economy is "mixed" — mixed because much of it is privately owned and the market-price mechanism remains important. Planning proliferated. France, some Scandinavian countries, and Holland have comprehensive plans, but most economic activities remain more or less in the private sector. The kind of programming done by the U.S. Council of Economic Advisers tries to put together the big economic facts, essentially to see how the economy is doing and to make policy suggestions for the consideration of the President, Congress, and the public. British White Papers and Japan's national plans have performed similar functions. Many other countries have different kinds of plans, with varying proportions of economic activity taken over or controlled by government. The scope of publicly owned corporations has greatly expanded — much beyond utilities like power and urban transportation — into railways, airlines, and airports, and in some countries even into industries like textiles and steel. Never have so many different socioeconomic experiments gone on simultaneously, and for this reason generalizations on policy formulation based on limited experience are likely to be wrong.

These approaches to national economic management have frequently been embodied in a comprehensive plan covering a number of years — five is popular — for a national, regional, or local level economy. These plans set agreed objectives, allocate productive resources to achieve these targets, and set forth policies and mechanisms for achieving them. The details may be so numerous that the "plan" requires many volumes to present. Objectives are set by the political leaders; they approve the plan targets which, in effect, means the choice of priorities, and they are responsible for their administration. The planners seemingly have the more purely technical jobs of allocating resources and selecting policies and instruments from feasible alternatives for achieving the agreed targets.

This kind of planning has had only limited successes and many failures. Too often the targets set forth are unrelated to societal realities and doomed to be stillborn.

There are many reasons for failing to be realistic in putting together a plan for an entire economy, with its thousands of component parts — locally, regionally, nationally, and internationally. Formal internal consistency has often been obtained by spurious precision — figures "cooked" to fit together because accurate figures were unavailable and those available did not fit. More important, planning on the national level has usually been regarded as a specialized economic exercise, even though it involves all aspects of society. Often it has not even involved all of economic science and experience, tending to gloss over monetary aspects like the availability and use of savings and the effects of persistent inflation. Political leaders tend often to be excessively impressed by figures, particularly if supplied by experts. Erroneous figures are the responsibility of their manufacturers. The political leaders could, however, have judged more carefully whether the means employed to implement the plan seemed realistic socially, politically, and administratively; they should have been able to judge whether the changes in society required to implement the plan were feasible. However, in practice, neither the political leaders nor their closest advisers have been able to give the plans the kind of detailed scrutiny needed to make such judgments. Too often, it has been easier to accept a plan, expecting that it will not be implemented, than to try to make it realistic or to see to its implementation. To do otherwise requires the direct involvement of political leaders in the planning process and implementation — an involvement which is most and frequently deemed impossibly demanding.

Thus it is obvious that I do not envisage that the national strategy needed to deal with basic social and economic ills is the more widespread use of planning techniques as hitherto practiced. A growing number of experienced national planners now seek radically different approaches. Persistent inflation can be tackled successfully only if it is part of an effort to meet basic social needs. Therefore, strategy planning for this purpose must include not only unemployment, hard-core and general, but also family planning, pollution, conservation of raw materials, health, education, housing, drugs, crime, problem children, urban decay. When these problems and needs are seen together, the whole approach of planning "from the top" by national planners removed from regional and local conditions comes even more into question.

Planning for social problems first requires identification of the basic ones; these are best discovered at the grass roots level. The selection of available or possible practical means for handling these problems can then follow. Having identified the problems and the feasible means, it is then possible to discuss how much can be done and, from this, to derive feasible targets and objectives. This approach encompasses all that we know, and all the techniques employed in the many areas of knowledge involved.

Such plans would not come into existence except as the reflection of the needs expressed by people, in their private organizations and through their political and social leaders at every level, and their judgments as to what is desirable and possible by way of policies and programs. Being political and social, it could often be sloppy, incomplete, literally inconsistent, and uncertain; but it would be realistically vital, viable, and visible — not to be put into desk drawers or file cabinets. From this process the strategy for dealing with societal needs can emerge.

Each group and political leader starts with existing answers. The national government would be expected to give its overall views. Regional and local authorities would express their views. All levels of government would interact with private organizations and with individuals. Governmental decisions would realistically reflect this continuing interaction and therefore are likely to be rough and ready. The process may sound like what happens now, but it differs greatly. The public participates and, most important, it can get what is promised. As social and economic problems are tackled simultaneously and we improve the methods of analysis and learn more how to interrelate goals and available means, the process will become increasingly more orderly and more efficient.

(5) Mechanisms and Institutions to Achieve Objectives

The need for national political leadership and coordination in achieving and implementing this strategy may suggest the need for change in governmental structures and procedures and probably new institutions. Most important will be the relations between private individuals and these institutions. In a pluralistic society, many institutions which could be involved exist already, and more could come into being. Whether and where to place the relative emphasis on personal initiative and private freedom as opposed to governmental authority and control will be part of the never-ending debate on what strategy should be employed to deal with the basic socioeconomic problems. Each country will provide its own answers, and change them repeatedly over time. As seen in the pursuit of full-employment goals, the most important element is widespread acceptance, as a top national objective, of the elimination of inflationary expectations; with this acceptance, public and private institutions will be constantly on the alert on how to accomplish this or prevent regression.

However governmental machinery is adapted, it should be multidisciplinary and intimately related to day-to-day policies. It may bear some resemblance to planning agencies, councils of economic advisers, and other similar existing institutions. It should, however, be modeled in terms of needs and practicality. It must be organically linked to the political process; it must not administer, but neither must it merely admonish or advise. It may take the form of a new sort of "kitchen cabinet" or privy council. It may rely very heavily on existing private institutions. But its aim would be to make the political leaders of nations, regions, or localities capable of heading administrations that have frightfully difficult and immensely important new social and economic duties. Experimentation and setbacks will be inevitable, but need not mean failure of the strategic approach. It does involve dedication to problem solving, using all available private as well as public mechanisms, and a determination to minimize bureaucratic power building.

22

The Ordering of Priorities

Selective Demand Management to Eliminate
Persistent Inflation

Against the above background for guides to action, we can
consider the economic aspects of choosing priorities to
achieve the elimination of persistent inflation. What is
needed is a set of rules for selective demand management
designed to overcome persistent inflation and inflationary expectations.

Before any ordering of priorities must come the decision
to eliminate inflationary expectations by ending persistent
inflation. This, as seen, is approached by a combination of
activities: identifying the social and economic causes of persistent inflation, deciding what changes are desired and pro-
ceeding to tackle these bottlenecks as systematically as
conditions permit. The principal difficulty lies in that
success requires a systematic sustained effort of years and
therefore what is done will have to be of a character that
would not be disturbed by changes in government. In this
sense, the achievement of the elimination of persistent infla-

tion *must* be a nonpartisan effort. It must be at least as non-partisan as the commitment to full employment.

The essential ingredient of demand management is the recognition that resources are limited. These resources can be seen as a limited capacity to produce goods and services. The capacity can be increased by certain economic activities like new investment, new mines and oilfields, additions to the labor force, and improved human skills. The resources can also be seen as a limited flow of goods and services resulting from the economic process. Demand management should aim to improve the stock of resources to enhance future productive capacity, to achieve the best possible flow of goods and services from present capacity, and to distribute this flow in some equitable manner. These aims can be achieved without causing persistent inflation. Under noninflationary conditions, this is not too hard to do. Demand management designed to end persistent inflation has, however, the critical, very difficult task in many countries of first eliminating inflationary expectations. The suggestions made herein are particularly addressed to this problem. They emphasize the importance of selectivity in management of demand.

The flow of goods and services is used for both consumption and investment. Government and public bodies provide some consumption such as education, publicly owned transportation facilities, and other utilities like electricity and water. Private firms provide the great bulk of consumption, such as food, clothing, automobiles, and plumbing repair services. To maintain the capacity to produce these consumption goods and services, both the public and private sectors engage in investment activities. Demand management thus has to deal with all kinds of consumption and investment activities, public and private. It has to be aware of the operation of both the market mechanism and the activities of every level of government. It cannot make believe that there are more goods and services to be distributed than will actually be available; it cannot pretend that it is providing for future capacity to produce when it rejects public and private investment in order to meet current consumption. This is painfully obvious but, too often, societies act as though these self-evident propositions could be ignored.

The Priorities

In view of this basic scarcity compared with demand, a clear pattern of priorities needs to be set up. First, the government must allocate national resources to meet those responsibilities it has accepted and it must make this decision realistically; above all, it must be successful in meeting its announced commitments. Second, it must take care of additional important public needs — a first-rate civil service, basic and applied research in areas where the private sector cannot assume the risks involved, fixed obligations such as the repayment of debt, and, possibly, defense. Third, it must encourage necessary productive investment. Fourth, it can decide on the allocation of remaining resources to consumption, both public and private. These decisions can be essentially seen as the choice between consumption and all other allocations in the developed world and between investment and other allocations in the developing countries. Let us now look at each of these priorities in turn.

First Priority: Governmental Commitments

Once the socioeconomic needs which a government has accepted as its responsibility have been identified, it will have to decide how much of its country's resources to allocate to meet them. At present the choice seems often to be among expenditures within the government's budget — education or housing or health. Often, only little is found from looking at different budget expenditures to see which can be reduced or eliminated to make room for higher-priority public expenditures. Fundamentally, because private consumption is large in the total use of output, the choice in the developed countries should be between the total of these public expenditures and the entire range of private consumption. In the developing countries, consumption is also a very large proportion of the whole, but because of widespread poverty there is little room for future compression, even assuming total output continues to increase. Therefore, in the low-income countries the choice is between top-priority governmental expenditures and other investments. If public expenditures for these purposes are so great that private consumption or investment in the developing countries cannot, or should not, be compressed sufficiently to accommodate them, governments should reconsider them. They must do all possible to fulfill accepted responsibilities. This could result in the clean-cut elimination of some government responsibilities. This is much preferable to accepting a responsibility and then failing to fulfill it. Examples of such failures are found everywhere: in poverty programs, public housing, education, health facilities, old-age support, child care. High-priority governmental responsibilities must either cease to be responsibilities or be met. To meet them, governments should not have to muscle the requisite expenditures into the line after other needs; they should have first priority. Whoever is part of the decision-making process must understand in accepting these governmental responsibilities, that they cannot be defaulted. Governments cannot otherwise hope to regain their greatly needed credibility with their people.

Second Priority: Other Governmental Needs

Having given top consideration to these priority expenditures in allocating the economy's entire resources, the government would then determine its additional needs. Again, it would approach this from the viewpoint that whatever is allocated for its own purposes is basically at the expense of consumption in the developed countries and investment in the less developed countries.

Governmental needs should be calculated on the assumption that a first-rate civil service equipped to handle modern governmental responsibilities is required, not only on the national but also on the state or regional and local levels. High-priority governmental expenditures should also include the funding of needed basic and applied research and development in areas in which the private sector cannot be expected to do the job. It must also include fixed obligations, like payments of debt. Issues like the redundancy of civil servants in some sectors, important in many countries, should be posed publicly as the choice they require — between keeping these redundant civil servants or otherwise providing income for them and the consumption or investment of the entire community — as well as in terms of percentages of total budgetary expenditures, budgetary deficits, increases in the money supply. Governments may choose for political or humanitarian reasons to keep redundant civil servants, but the cost to society would then be more clearly seen.

Defense Expenditures: Having taken the first two steps, the governments would then have committed an important share of the total output and met the highest priorities in most countries. In many countries, however, there is the special question of major defense expenditures. This question involves domestic and international political judgments and personal value systems. It is clear, however, that at present whatever is agreed on for military expenditures is automatically given a very high priority. It is less clear that defense expenditures are not necessarily at the expense of other top-priority expenditures; they could and should be recognized as being at the expense of general consumption in the developed countries and investment in the developing countries. This is especially important where defense expenditures are very large and even more so in low-income countries.

Third Priority: Investment

The next step for governments would be to consider the allocation of remaining output for the still uncovered portion of activities — remaining investment and consumption. This remainder would include both private and public activities. In the developed countries, it is likely to be large enough to lend itself to more subdivisions as between higher and lower priority investment and consumption.

Then, third on the list of priorities ought to be necessary investment. The relative weights and composition of private and public investment would, of course, vary greatly among countries and within them over time. Judgments on what and how much is desirable would come out of the process of developing a national strategy. They would reflect continuing interaction between government and the private sector. Again, the choice would be seen as between these investments and what remains for consumption once the first two top-priority governmental needs have been met. Again, there may be a need for a trade-off between productive investment and consumption, with productive investment being usually regarded as having the higher priority of claims on the limited resources of the country.

In the developing countries, there may well be an acute painful dilemma. Productive investment is essential to overcome the low levels of output and productivity which, in turn, hamper attacks on social and other economic problems. These low levels of output often mean widespread poverty and therefore little savings — either in absolute amounts or as percentages of total output of the economy. Governments having committed resources to the top priorities, there may be little left over for productive investment, whether public or private. In effect, necessary consumption will frequently have to be satisfied, irrespective of the repercussions for investment and future output. This gives special importance to good economic management of available resources in low-income countries. Widespread poverty makes much-needed and practical productive investment, in effect, the residual claimant on a developing country's resources. This helps explain why increments to available resources through private capital imports and official development assistance are so important for the poorer countries.

Because of the higher output and incomes in industrialized economies, investment need not be sacrificed because the government is fulfilling its top-priority commitments. In this sense, consumption rather than investment may be regarded in an industrialized country as a residual claimant on its resources.

Fourth Priority: Consumption

From Consumerism to Consumption: Having decided on the above allocations for high-priority purposes, what remains in a developed country is the productive capacity to provide goods and services for consumption. In dealing with consumption, we are dealing with the largest slice of any economy. It is always much more than 50 percent of the whole, and may well be closer to 80 and 90 percent. It is this sector that modern industrialized societies need to explore most closely to see whether resources now used for consumption can be spared to find the resources needed to meet agreed societal responsibilities.

The basic aim is to achieve a satisfactory pattern of consumption to replace present-day consumerism. In considering consumption and how it might, if needed, be reduced as well as altered, it is tempting to set up firm criteria for choice.

Governments have often had to make this kind of decision. Controlled economies do it all the time. In wartime, most governments decide what is necessary and discourage other consumption. They adopt combinations of price and wage controls, material allocations for production, consumer rationing, prohibitions on production and sales, price incentives and disincentives, and other direct controls. War conditions dicate cutbacks and the government takes responsibility for deciding what is produced and consumed and what is not. In peacetime, extensive domestic controls are rare. They require strong public acceptance, which is not likely to be forthcoming, even if otherwise they might be favored.

But there is a rich experience of governments' using controls in peacetime to help manage their balance of payments. Most governments of the world at one time or another have used exchange controls to limit expenditures on imports and other foreign payments. In doing so, they had to establish criteria for allocating scarce foreign exchange. Needed investments and "essential" consumption have usually had the highest priorities (in addition to servicing of government or government-guaranteed external debt). Essential consumption varies depending on local conditions. It nearly always includes some foodstuffs and pharmaceuticals. It frequently includes newsprint and educational materials. At the other end, it nearly always greatly restricts or even prohibits, by government controls or by higher taxes, large, expensive automobiles and other consumer durables which may be regarded as luxuries. It is also likely to curb extensive foreign-holiday trips, while permitting limited amounts of travel for medical treatment and education abroad.

Easy decisions in principle are often very difficult decisions in detail. What is a needed pharmaceutical and how much should there be? What books, journals, and newspapers are "educational"? Are large automobiles imported to use in carrying on tourist business attractive to foreigners to be regarded as luxuries? Corresponding difficulties arise in deciding what is needed for agricultural and industrial production. It is no wonder, on the one hand, that exchange licensing is often mismanaged and leads to great corruption and, on the other, that governments are often very pleased to be able to relax restrictions and get out of this impossible business of minute detailed guessing of the demands of people and firms.

Furthermore, demands are altered by the very restrictions. For example, governments may decide to limit new tire imports, but this results in demands for old tires, equipment and materials to rebuild tires or to manufacture tires locally. Less obviously, luxury imports are greatly reduced or stopped, but local businesses supplying substitute pleasures flourish. Domestic materials and labor are used which might otherwise be producing other goods and services, including some for export.

I have had too much experience with exchange controls not to be highly skeptical of governments' ability to make detailed choices respecting consumption and implementation, and to deal with the unexpected and unwanted side effects. However, the elimination of persistent inflation requires in a number, if not all, of the industrialized countries that certain kinds of consumption be reduced from the levels that would otherwise prevail. In some, this may only mean that less of future increases in national output be used for consumption; in others, it may require actual reduction in consumption. Much will depend on what governmental expenditures are regarded as "musts," how much additional resources is required in a country to obtain the needed excellence in public service (including reduction of corruption to tolerable levels), and how much must be devoted to high-priority investment.

In approaching this problem, the distinction between public consumption and private consumption is not as meaningful as it might appear to be! High-priority government-accepted consumption responsibilities have already been taken care of. Some, like education, training of potentially employable hard-core unemployed, welfare for the neediest, may be supplied by government. Others may involve the private sector but require governmental expenditures for subsidies, or losses of government revenues through tax rebates or reduction or elimination of certain taxes; subsidized housing, transport, and food are examples here.

Prices for consumer goods and services change unevenly and oddly as they reflect the impact of persistent inflation. Hence, restraints on consumption cannot be guided by relative price changes for different products and services under conditions of persistent inflation. To increase the supply of goods which rise the most in price may seem sensible; increased supply should bring down prices. But these goods may be unimportant to the community at large, and increased supplies would waste scarce productive resources. It may instead make sense to restrain demand for such goods and services.

Role of Government: There are two basic ways of approaching the role of government in influencing consumption: one is to make all consumption sufficiently more expensive to compress the total, leaving the composition of consumption essentially up to the interplay of consumer preferences, advertising, credit availability, and the other factors affecting producers' activities operating in the market; the second is to try to influence the composition as well as the totality of consumption. The latter can also be done primarily through the market mechanism, using devices like taxes and consumer credits, or through direct governmental controls.

Thus, people have to choose between a general compression of consumption or a selective compression, having the pattern of consumption largely determined by the political process. However, if the overall strategy and the process of its implementation involve open debate with clearly stated issues and alternatives, people may be less leery of the political process making such choices; more people will have influenced the choices made. Administrative feasibilities may, however, prove an overwhelming obstacle in some countries.

The case against influencing the composition of consumption is fairly easy to make. Experience shrieks warnings against governments trying to decide detailed consumption. In the first place, it can be an administrative can of worms if it aims at detailed distinctions; enforcement is most difficult and business may find compliance nearly impossible. If deciding details of consumption is part of comprehensive economic controls, it may result in gray uniformity, shoddy quality, and chronic imbalances between supply and demand. For many it is one of the most disagreeable aspects of the Orwellian society, closely related to feelings of personal freedom and self-respect. However, as will be noted shortly, a desired change in the composition of consumption can be effected in a manner compatible with consumer choice exercised through the market mechanism. In any case, the compression of consumption might by itself create pressures to move consumption demand away from present-day consumerism.

The case for influencing the composition of consumption is that it could improve the consumption of the great majority of people. Until persistent inflation is finally eliminated, consumerism is likely to continue to be strong, with production and investment accordingly pointed that way. If high-priority needs have already been met, consumerism may not be too harmful. Nonetheless, it is at the expense of the large majority of people, who will have to choose from the distorted supply of goods and services until persistent inflation is eliminated. Thus influencing the composition of consumption could sooner provide more of the kind of goods and services needed by people in middle and lower income groups.

This could be done so as to minimize, if not eliminate, the dangers of bureaucratic substitution for consumer choice. If done successfully, it could release large quantities of resources to meet higher-priority consumption and investment needs, as well as governmental commitments. Consumption demands for most people could be better met, while virtually no one would need feel deprived in achieving desired consumption.

Selectivity in consumption can be approached in many

different ways. One could distinguish "necessities" from "luxuries." Among other criteria which could be used to select a pattern of consumption are the impact of producing different goods and services on existing social problems like hard-core unemployment and inadequate housing; efficiency in use of productive resources; conservation of exhaustible materials, minimizing or eliminating pollution; labor use; and, if necessary, rehabilitation and maintenance of accumulated social and private capital and emphasis on commodities which are durable. Influenced by criteria formulated in the process of public debate, the market mechanism can encourage consumption and thereby guide production and investment.

In practice, these approaches to compressing consumption — general vs. selective constraint — would probably be intermingled and, as in many other cases, would vary greatly from country to country and within countries over time. Nothing is inevitable in any choice and all contain strong subjective elements reflecting personal or societal value systems. If it is kept in mind that these decisions are highly individual and personal, and that experts and government officials can contribute their knowledge and wisdom in making decisions, but are not qualified to make most of them by themselves, the chances of major errors are reduced.

Of course, I am assuming that as long as world consumption and investment needs and demands remain much above output capacity, there is no real likelihood of deliberately cutting back or restraining output in the industrial workshops of the world. We may expect strong emphasis on more careful use of exhaustible raw materials, environmental controls, and so forth; but this will affect the method of production, not diminish the need for much increased output and capacity. The concept of excess capacity is relevant in the modern world only if we ignore that 60 to 70 percent of mankind lives at below-human standards of consumption. There may be objections to the United States' and other industrial economies' using much of the world's exhaustible materials for their small fraction of the world's population. There should be much less objection if the global distribution of that production were to change so that much more were consumed by lower-income groups and lower-income countries.

Mechanism to Alter Consumption: The institutions in government and the private sector to make the societal choices of consumption already largely exist. But their activities will change. Implementing choices will also involve all people, particularly organized groups and institutions, private and governmental. Private groups already interact daily with government at all levels. If the social and economic causes of persistent inflation were to be tackled along the lines I suggest, new public and private institutions are likely to evolve and new dimensions are likely to be added to existing groups, such as private consumer groups, environmentalists, and senior citizens.

Where institutional arrangements are already deficient, for example, where there is need for more extensive banking facilities or a capital market, the new needs would heighten pressures to create new institutions, or improve existing ones. But the major changes would be essentially in the policies

governing these institutions. Budgets scheduling government expenditure and taxation, and monetary measures
affecting money and credit would be, as now, the principal
vehicles. Their use, however, would be different.

In many cases, the changes needed would not be major; in
others, they would need to be. The lesser changes would
constrain consumption by a combination of credit restraints,
particularly on consumer credit, and increased incentives to
save, like marked increases in interest on savings deposits or
government savings bonds. The greater changes in consumption can be achieved by a combination of higher taxes
and monetary restraints on consumer credit. Much would
depend on public tolerance of further tax increases as well as
the existence of effective monetary alternatives.

If higher taxes were required and feasible, they could
weigh mainly on either personal income or business income,
or a combination of both; alternatively there could be more
use of indirect, sales or value-added taxes. Any tax at a
uniform rate is obviously easier and less onerous to pay for a
person with a higher income than one with lower income.
Such taxes are usually regarded as "regressive." But there
are ways of overcoming this, and of compensating lower-
income groups by more generous treatment for them in
payment of direct taxes on income. Similarly, productive
investments could be encouraged by tax incentives, or discouraged. These are all within the capabilities of the present
system; only their redirection to new ends would be
required.

Taxation devices could, however, also be used in novel
ways. For example, a sales or value-added tax might be made

progressive, not regressive, by differentiating the rates. Deciding to do so would have to be related to judgments on how far it is desired to encourage the consumption of certain goods and services and discourage that of others, and how administratively feasible any such tax might be. The rates could be set according to income levels of likely consumers of the particular products or services, but other social and economic criteria could also be given weight. For example, tax rates on expensive automobiles might be much higher than those on less expensive or smaller ones. The rates might reflect not only the desired shift in consumption, but also the car's contribution to pollution, highway usage, and traffic congestion. Taxes on gasoline with fewer pollutants might be reduced, while those on high-octane gasoline were raised. Tolls on highways to cities might be higher during rush hours than otherwise, or, as is seen in some places, lower for leaving a city than for entering. Cars with more passengers might be charged less in tolls or public parking fees than cars with fewer passengers. The same approach or variants on it could be applied to housing, food, entertainment, clothing, hotel accommodation, cosmetics. Conversely, greater tax allowances could be made for people in average and below-average income groups, for essential medical needs, special schooling, training for new jobs.

It would be possible to differentiate business and personal income taxes according to the way in which the income was earned. This could, of course, become very complicated. Yet certain possibilities are obvious: higher income taxes on earnings from renting luxury apartments, or on earnings from producing specific commodities. In tandem with progressive taxes on consumption, demand and supply might well change markedly.

All of these are, however, great inducements to tax avoidance — as always tax lawyers will benefit. But it is impossible to have taxes without attempts to avoid or evade them. And perhaps it compliments a community to say that its tax lawyers are busy; people are taking tax law seriously, not simply ignoring it. The aim should be to have a tax system which is equitable and reasonably efficient and, simultaneously, to use it to help end persistent inflation. To end persistent inflation the methods used must be socially and politically acceptable. Tax avoidance makes life more complicated for some, more profitable for others, but it need not defeat these aims of tax legislation.

Parallel actions are possible in the credit field. Special credit facilities are already given for lower-income housing, and the terms of the credits do seem to affect activity in the construction industry; often, however, they do not stimulate building of lower-income housing. Too often changes are seriously delayed because of bureaucratic difficulties. This does not mean that the approach is wrong, rather that it has been inadequately implemented. Private builders do respond to changing market conditions and investment opportunities; special subsidy credit arrangements must be made in recognition of this fact. Only then can priority needs be met.

Special credit terms need to be modified quickly as conditions change, and the process of governmental clearances must be simplified if special credits are to achieve their objectives. Credit for consumer durables could vary requirements as to down-payment, maturity, or interest rates to discourage too frequent changes in model and encourage maintenance. Changes in consumer credit availability could be powerful tools in slowing down consumerism. More special credit facilities could be created for maintenance purposes, whether of consumer durables or of housing. Consumer groups could advise on availability of such special credits as well as on products to be purchased. Some private banks are already taking initiatives in this field and doing imaginative things. "Truth-in-lending" legislation can keep purchasers from being cheated or, at least, inform borrowers of the total cost of credit. We need to ensure that such help is widely available, particularly to lower- and middle-income people.

Closely related to taxation and credit measures are devices which induce more savings. Indeed, to encourage savings it is possible to give exceptional income tax treatment for investments in financial assets like savings bonds. By such measures more resources would be available to meet the established higher-priority consumption and investment needs. This can be particularly important in countries already experiencing taxpayer revolts against higher taxes. Higher taxes may be necessary in many countries to avoid inflationary financing of budgets (government borrowing from the central bank or commercial banking system), but beyond a certain point taxes can give way to increased savings and accomplish the same ends.

All of these approaches rely essentially on the price-market mechanism. By taxation and subsidies, they change relative prices; by changes in credit and inducements to saving, they affect relative demand. They mean, for many, a willingness to be open-minded about strongly held views on taxation and use of the banking system. But the effects of persistent inflation demand that feasible lines of attack not be deployed in advance of most careful consideration of their effects and alternatives.

As emphasized before, however attractive ideas like these may be to some, tests of administrative practicality must always be severely applied. The less detailed the differentiation among products and services in applying different tax and credit measures, the more feasible they are likely to prove. It would also be possible to have wage and profit policies which, in effect, induce higher wages and profits in selected activities. To the extent that the national order of priorities worked, wages and profits would be higher over time in more productive industries.

The discussion and choice of strategies and priorities suggested above would presumably largely take place around these issues of taxation, credit policies, and wage and profit policies designed to influence the level and pattern of consumption. It is these changes which make room for the other activities in the fields of public expenditures and taxation. These proposed measures would raise fundamental questions about priorities through the back door of asking what consumption people are prepared to sacrifice to fulfill high-priority government expenditure and investment needs. At every level of society and government, such discussions would be concrete and meaningful. People would focus on these issues and have strong incentives to organize themselves to influence the outcome. For example, consumer groups would be much more important because the questions on consumption would be much more searching and affect many more deeply than present-day activities of consumer groups. Laborer and producer groups would be vitally affected — some firms or industries would be adversely affected and manpower-adjustment policies similar to those used in import-liberalization cases might well have to be used.

More important, it would be recognized that the implementation of strategies to eliminate persistent inflation is not only difficult, though warranted, but, like a strategy for social and economic development to achieve the structural transformation of societies, it must be conceived over a considerable number of years, have the flexibility to change and the public support to endure. Indeed, if the effort to eliminate persistent inflation is successful, many of the bottlenecks to achieving the desired structural transformation will also have been broken.

23

It Can Be Done

Much has to be decided and done to implement a societal approach to inflation. Of critical importance is provoking sufficient public interest and concern to sustain public support over the period of years needed for programs to eliminate persistent inflation. If the political leadership and public understanding exist, then work in overcoming persistent inflation can be begun and sustained. If not, the first task is one of education and persuasion.

The approach suggested herein would transform modern societies. In this context, achievement of noninflationary conditions, while also attaining other agreed national objectives and priorities, is the touchstone. Available resources would then be realistically appraised, their potential fully utilized. Public and private consumption would be altered so as to achieve the maximum general satisfaction compatible with the fullest use of available resources and their potential. Persistent inflation, however manifest, would then be evidence of bad errors in judgment or in execution; and continuation of such errors would be known to jeopardize the achievement of social and economic objectives.

If the basic causes of persistent inflation are not tackled, societal conditions can only get worse. If this happens in low-income countries, the price is paid by the already great majority of miserably poor inhabitants. If this happens in high-income countries, the price is paid by the large majority of people, or all, as the personal, social, and political tensions of modern societies do not exclude anyone.

No international economic system will survive the effects of the constant pummeling of persistent inflation. The domestic effects can become a cause of international friction because of their political consequences. Until now it has been a world of mismanaged economies, making progress despite these mistakes. It would take an ostrichlike optimist to believe that this progress can continue for long unless the fundamental problems are brought into focus and more success is achieved in solving them. We are called on to solve these problems in order to achieve viable societies in which prophecies of gloom will no longer be commonplace. This, unfortunately, is no forecast that effective policies will be taken. Fortunately, strong pressures move us to do something effective, and the means to do it are available.

Index

Index